R
Designs fo

WIRKLICHKEIT BOOKS

Edited by
JONAS VON LENTHE

TABLE OF CONTENTS

INTRODUCTION

In December 1955, when the Council of Europe selected a European flag consisting of twelve yellow stars arranged in a circle on a blue background, it was simultaneously rejecting over 150 flag designs that had been submitted since the Council was founded in 1949. The design drafts came from all over the world; however, most of them were submitted by men from West Germany and France.

All the proposals were based on the assumption that European unity was the model for the future, though opinions differed as to which symbols might best unite Europe. The proposals ranged from the Swiss cross (Switzerland serving as a model for Europe here due to its peaceful multilingualism), to Strasbourg's coat of arms (a symbol of Franco-German reconciliation and European post-war achievements), to the star (a popular flag symbol and US reference), all the way to the abstract map (an attempt to situate Europe territorially).

The proposals are not without their share of imperialist fantasies: in many cases – as evidenced by the letters accompanying the design drafts – the flag becomes a symbol of the continent's cultural superiority over the rest of the world, and thus a testimony to the colonialist society of the Europe of the time.

The angles and motives for pursuing the idea of a united Europe differed drastically from one another: it was to be found both in the socialist-dominated resistance movements in fascist Italy, as well as in conservative and decidedly Eurocentric circles of the time. While the former had the liberation of the working classes in mind, the latter were concerned

5

about the dwindling importance of Europe in world affairs. The only point on which they agreed was that European nationalisms could only be kept in check by joining together to form a union, and that this was the only way to prevent another war.

The European flag was therefore both a project of continental peace and a means of establishing a boundary to the outside world – an aspect also characteristic of Europe today, where the dismantling of internal borders goes hand in hand with increasing barricading against foreigners and migrants.

On a symbolic level too, the flag is used to delineate: as an early form of branding "Europe", it made the idea of a united Europe visually distinguishable and competitive vis-à-vis a national order for the first time, marking the beginning of a campaign of persuasion and advertising for its own cause that continues to this day.

The design of the European flag is generally credited to Arsène Heitz, a former employee of the Council of Europe's postal service, who submitted more than 30 variations of the flag (see p. 118-139). However, to this day the question of the flag's authorship remains controversial: the concept of stars arranged in a circle has been documented in several design drafts, including those by the Hamburg lawyer Hanno F. Konopath (see p. 110-117). Paul M. G. Levy, then Director of the Press and Information Service of the Council of Europe, also claimed that the circle of stars was his idea. Yellow stars on a blue background also appear in a design by the Spanish diplomat and writer Salvador de Madariaga (see p. 93), where they mark the locations of European capitals.[1]

The rejected flag designs are a record of the continent's self-image during a period of course-setting with regard to European integration, which may be attributed a particularly high degree of elasticity in terms of its historical development perspectives.[2] The drawings in this book have been grouped according to motifs in order to highlight the ideas and trends circulating at the time. For example, designs featuring a sun, a star or the Strasbourg city coat of arms each have a separate section dedicated to them. The only exceptions are drafts by individuals who have sent a particularly large number of proposals to the Council of Europe: in such cases, all drawings by the respective creator have been combined. The text passages below the illustrations are taken from letters sent to the Council of Europe along with the respective proposals. They provide valuable background information about the motives and symbolism of the artistic creation or insight into the creator's private life.[3]

The flag drawings are accompanied by an essay by the poet and writer Marie Rotkopf, who provides a sharp analysis of the current political situation in Europe.

[1]
See Carlo Curti Gialdino, *The Symbols of the European Union: origin of the design for the European flag*, www.cvce.eu/obj/carlo_curti_gialdino_the_symbols_of_the_european_union_origin_of_the_design_for_the_european_flag-en-df9f9dde-98a3-461b-a8a8-8f9c13012343.html (accessed 29.8.2020)

[2]
See Achim Trunk, *Europa, ein Ausweg. Politische Eliten und europäische Identität in den 1950er Jahren*, (Munich 2007), p. 11.

[3]
The letter by Hanno F. Konopath cited on page 110 ff. is dated 1958. In it he refers to his flag designs from 1952.

This publication aims to contribute to a structural understanding of Europe today, both through the essay and the historical documents. Above all, it reveals the ambivalences and continuities of so-called European unity. Finally, the heterogeneous archive material, published for the first time in this volume, illustrates the historical constructedness of the current situation, therefore highlighting the potential to participate in shaping it.

Jonas von Lenthe, June 2020

EINLEITUNG

Als der Europarat im Dezember 1955 eine Europaflagge, bestehend aus zwölf im Kreis angeordneten gelben Sternen auf blauem Grund, auswählte, entschied er sich im selben Moment gegen über 150 Flaggenentwürfe, die seit der Gründung des Europarats im Jahr 1949 eingereicht worden waren. Die Entwürfe kamen aus der ganzen Welt, die meisten von ihnen stammten allerdings von Männern aus Westdeutschland und Frankreich.

Allen Entwürfen liegt die Annahme zugrunde, dass die europäische Einheit das Modell der Zukunft sei, während die Vorstellungen darüber auseinander gingen, welche Symbole Europa vereinen könnten.

Die Vorschläge reichen vom Schweizer Kreuz (die Schweiz ist hier wegen ihrer friedlichen Vielsprachigkeit Vorbild für Europa) über das Wappen von Straßburg (Zeichen der deutsch-französischen Aussöhnung und europäischen Nachkriegserrungenschaften) und den Stern (beliebtes Flaggensymbol und USA-Referenz) bis hin zur abstrahierten Landkarte (Versuch einer territorialen Verortung Europas).

Auch sind die Entwürfe nicht frei von imperialistischen Fantasien: In einigen Fällen – das belegen den Entwürfen beiliegende Briefe – wird die Flagge zum Symbol für die kulturelle Überlegenheit des Kontinents gegenüber dem Rest der Welt und somit zum Zeugnis der kolonialistischen Gesellschaft des damaligen Europas.

Die Idee eines vereinten Europas wurde von verschiedenen Seiten und aus verschiedenen Motivationen heraus verfolgt: Sie fand sich sowohl in den sozialistisch geprägten Widerstandsbewegungen im faschistischen Italien als auch in konservativen und überzeugt eurozentristischen Kreisen der Zeit. Während erstere nicht zuletzt die Befreiung der Arbeiterklasse im Blick hatten, fürchteten letztere die schwindende Bedeutung Europas im Weltgeschehen. Einig waren sie sich lediglich in einem Punkt: dass die europäischen Nationalismen allein durch einen Zusammenschluss zur Gemeinschaft im Zaum gehalten werden könnten und nur so ein erneuter Krieg vermieden werden könne.

Die Europaflagge war also in gleichem Maße ein Projekt des kontinentalen Friedens wie auch ein Mittel der Abgrenzung nach außen – eine Struktur, die auch für das heutige Europa bezeichnend ist: So geht der Abbau der Grenzen im Inneren einher mit einer zunehmenden Verbarrikadierung gegenüber Fremden und Migrant*innen. Und auch auf symbolischer Ebene wird die Flagge verwendet, um abzugrenzen: Als frühe Form des Europa-Brandings machte sie die Idee eines vereinten Europas erstmals visuell unterscheidbar und konkurrenzfähig gegenüber einer nationalen Ordnung und stellte den Anfang einer bis heute währenden Überzeugungs- und Werbekampagne für die eigene Sache dar.

Als Urheber der Europaflagge gilt gemeinhin Arsène Heitz, ein damaliger Angestellter der Poststelle des Europarats, der über 30 Flaggenvariationen einreichte (siehe S. 118-139). Jedoch ist die Autorschaft bis heute umstritten: Die Idee der im Kreis angeordneten Sterne taucht nachweislich in mehreren Entwürfen auf, so unter anderem in denen des Hamburger Juristen Hanno F. Konopath (siehe S. 110-117). Auch behauptete Paul M. G. Levy, der damalige Direktor des Presse- und Informationsdienstes des Europarats, der Sternenkreis sei sein Einfall gewesen. Als Markierungen der europäischen Hauptstädte finden sich die gelben Sterne auf blauem Grund ebenfalls in einem Entwurf des spanischen Diplomaten und Schriftstellers Salvador de Madariaga (siehe S. 93).[1]

Die abgelehnten Flaggenentwürfe dokumentieren das Selbstbild des Kontinents in einer „Zeit der Weichenstellungen" der europäischen Integration, der „eine besonders hohe Elastizität der historischen Entwicklungsperspektiven zugesprochen werden"[2] kann. Um die zu dieser Zeit zirkulierenden Ideen und Trends herauszuarbeiten, sind die Zeichnungen im vorliegenden Buch nach Motiven geordnet. So bilden etwa solche mit einer Sonne, einem Stern oder dem Straßburger Stadtwappen je einen eigenen Abschnitt. Ausnahmen stellen lediglich die Entwürfe von einzelnen Personen dar, die besonders viele Vorschläge an den Europarat geschickt haben: In diesen Fällen sind alle Zeichnungen des jeweiligen Urhebers zusammengefasst.

1
Vgl. Carlo Curti Gialdino, *The Symbols of the European Union: origin of the design for the European flag*, www.cvce.eu/obj/carlo_curti_gialdino_the_symbols_of_the_european_union_origin_of_the_design_for_the_european_flag-en-df9f9dde-98a3-461b-a8a8-8f9c13012343.html (zuletzt aufgerufen am 29.8.2020)

2
Achim Trunk, *Europa, ein Ausweg. Politische Eliten und europäische Identität in den 1950er Jahren*, München: De Gruyter Oldenbourg, 2007, S. 11.

Die Textpassagen unter den Abbildungen sind den Briefen entnommen, die mit den jeweiligen Entwürfen an den Europarat gesendet wurden. Sie geben Auskunft über die Beweggründe und Symbolik des künstlerischen Erzeugnisses oder Einblick in das Privatleben der Person.[3]

Den Flaggenzeichnungen folgt ein Essay der Schriftstellerin und Dichterin Marie Rotkopf, die eine scharfe Analyse der heutigen politischen Situation Europas liefert.

Das vorliegende Buch – das Essay ebenso wie die historischen Dokumente – ist ein Beitrag zu einem strukturellen Verständnis für das heutige Europa. Dabei werden vor allem die Ambivalenzen und Kontinuitäten der sogenannten europäischen Einheit erkennbar. Nicht zuletzt verdeutlicht das heterogene und in diesem Band erstmals veröffentlichte Archivmaterial die historische Konstruiertheit der heutigen Situation und damit die Möglichkeit einer Mitgestaltung.

Jonas von Lenthe, Juni 2020

3
Der von Hanno Konopath zitierte Brief auf Seite 110 ff. ist von 1958 datiert. In diesem bezieht er sich auf seine Flaggenentwürfe von 1952.

AVANT-PROPOS

Lorsque le Conseil de l'Europe choisit en décembre 1955 un drapeau européen représentant douze étoiles jaunes disposées en cercle sur un fond bleu, il se décide en même temps contre plus de 150 autres propositions de drapeaux, qui furent envoyées depuis sa fondation en 1949. Les ébauches venaient du monde entier, cependant la plupart furent des projets d'hommes d'Allemagne de l'Ouest et de France.

Tous les projets partaient du principe que l'union européenne serait le modèle du futur, tandis que les conceptions divergeaient quant au symbole qui pourrait bien réunir l'Europe.

Les propositions allaient de la croix suisse – la Suisse, en raison de son exemple de multilinguisme pacifique – au blason de Strasbourg, signe de la réconciliation franco-allemande et des réalisations européennes d'après-guerre, en passant par l'étoile, symbole populaire apprécié et référence aux USA, jusqu'à la cartographie abstraite, tentative d'un encrage territorial européen.

Les ébauches ne sont pas non plus dénuées de fantasmes impérialistes : dans certains cas, comme l'attestent les lettres jointes aux dessins, le drapeau devient un symbole de la soi-disant supériorité culturelle du continent sur le reste du monde et témoigne ainsi de la société colonialiste de l'Europe de l'époque.

L'idée d'une Europe unie a été suivie par différents courants, emmenée par différentes motivations : on la trouvait aussi bien dans l'Italie fasciste, au sein des mouvements résistants socialistes, que dans les cercles conservateurs «eurocentriques» convaincus. Alors que les premiers visaient la libération de la classe ouvrière, les seconds craignaient le déclin de l'importance de l'Europe dans la marche et les affaires du monde. Mais tous étaient d'accord sur ce point: les nationalismes européens ne pourraient être contenus que grâce à l'union, pour former ensemble une communauté et ainsi le seul moyen d'éviter une nouvelle guerre.

Le drapeau européen était donc un projet de paix continentale et de la même façon, un dispositif de démarcation vis-à-vis du monde extérieur. Une structure qui est aussi révélatrice de l'Europe actuelle. Ainsi le démantèlement des frontières intérieures va de pair avec une mise en place croissante de barricades contre les « étrangers » et les migrants. Au niveau symbolique, le drapeau est également utilisé pour délimiter, baliser: comme forme première d'une image de marque, d'un branding européen, il rend d'abord visuellement reconnaissable l'idée d'une Europe unie, puis compétitive face à un ordre national, et représente le début, encore et toujours, d'une campagne de persuasion et de communication.

Arsène Heitz, ancien employé de la poste du Conseil de l'Europe, qui a soumis plus de 30 variantes de drapeau (voir p. 118-139), est généralement considéré comme l'auteur du drapeau européen. Cependant, la paternité est encore controversée aujourd'hui: l'idée des étoiles disposées en cercle apparaît manifestement dans plusieurs projets, dont ceux du juriste hambourgeois Hanno F. Konopath (voir p. 110-117). Paul M. G. Levy, alors directeur du Service de presse et d'information du Conseil de l'Europe, a également affirmé que le cercle d'étoiles venait de lui. Les étoiles jaunes sur fond bleu désignant les capitales européennes se trouvent aussi dans un dessin du diplomate et écrivain espagnol Salvador de Madariaga (voir p. 93).[1]

Les drapeaux refusés forment un autoportrait du continent à une époque clé de l'intégration européenne, à laquelle «une possibilité particulièrement élevée de perspectives historiques pouvait être attribuée».[2] Afin de rendre compte des idées et tendances qui circulaient à l'époque, les dessins sont classés selon leurs motifs. Ceux avec un soleil, une étoile ou le blason de la ville de Strasbourg forment chacun une partie distincte. Les seules exceptions sont les projets de personnes qui ont envoyé un nombre particulièrement important de propositions au Conseil de l'Europe : dans ces cas, tous les dessins de l'auteur respectif sont regroupés. Les passages de texte sous les esquisses sont tirés des lettres qui ont été envoyées au Conseil de l'Europe avec les projets. Ils fournissent des informations sur les motivations et la symbolique du résultat artistique ou simplement un aperçu de la vie privée de l'auteur.[3]

Les propositions de drapeaux sont suivies d'un essai de l'écrivaine et poète Marie Rotkopf, qui livre une analyse acérée de la situation politique actuelle en Europe.

1
Cf. Carlo Curti Gialdino, *The Symbols of the European Union: origin of the design for the European flag*, www.cvce.eu/obj/carlo_curti_gialdino_the_symbols_of_the_european_union_origin_of_the_design_for_the_european_flag-en-df9f9dde-98a3-461b-a8a8-8f9c13012343.html

2
Achim Trunk, *Europa, ein Ausweg. Politische Eliten und europäische Identität in den 1950er Jahren*, De Gruyter Oldenbourg, München 2007, S. 11.

3
La lettre citée par Hanno Konopath à la page 110 et suivantes est datée de 1958. Il y fait référence à ses dessins de drapeaux de 1952.

Ce livre – l'essai comme les documents historiques – veut contribuer à une compréhension
structurelle de l'Europe d'aujourd'hui. Les
continuités et ambivalences de la prétendue
unité européenne doivent être ainsi rendues
perceptibles. Enfin, l'hétérogénéité du matériel
d'archives publié pour la première fois expli-
cite et témoigne de la construction historique
de la situation actuelle et offre par conséquent
la possibilité d'y prendre part.

Jonas von Lenthe, juin 2020

THE REJECTED DESIGNS
FOR THE EUROPEAN FLAG

Camile Manné, Strasbourg, 1949

"The flag must be familiar to every European and help to unite the different national traditions. It must symbolise at once the end of the fratricidal wars which still ravage Europe, and the reconciliation of the principal antagonists of the 20th century, the Anglo-French Alliance on the one hand, and the Germans on the other."

DE „Die Flagge muss jedem Europäer vertraut sein und dazu beitragen, die verschiedenen nationalen Traditionen zu vereinen. Sie muss in gleichem Maße das Ende der Bruderkriege symbolisieren, die noch immer in Europa wüten, sowie die Versöhnung der Hauptgegner des 20. Jahrhunderts, der englisch-französischen Allianz auf der einen und der Deutschen auf der anderen Seite."

FR « L'unification de l'Europe devra trouver son expression symbolique en un drapeau dans lequel se reconnaîtront toutes les anciennes nations qui feront partie de la communauté européenne en voie de création. Ce drapeau devra être le miroir dans lequel se reflèteront tous les anciens drapeaux des nations Européennes. Il devra être familier à chaque Européen et aider à l'unification des différentes tendances nationales. »

unidentified

August Vincent, Monte Carlo, 1950

"The flag that I envisage has a white cross in the middle to emphasise the fact that Europe is a Christian continent. The colours red, blue, green and orange are to be found in most European flags."

DE   „Die Fahne, die mir vorschwebt, hat in der Mitte ein weißes Kreuz, um die Tatsache zu betonen, dass Europa ein christlicher Kontinent ist. Die Farben Rot, Blau, Grün und Orange kommen in den meisten europäischen Flaggen vor."

FR   « Le drapeau que j'ai en tête a une croix blanche au centre, afin de souligner le fait que l'Europe est un continent chrétien. Les couleurs rouge, bleue, verte et orange sont toutes des couleurs qui sont incarnées dans la plupart des drapeaux européens. »

unidentified

Joseph Oberson-Bagnolet, Bordeaux, 1952

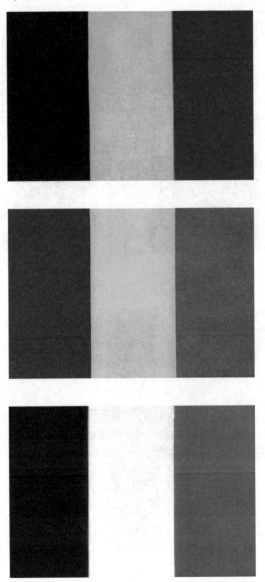

unidentified

unidentified

Walther Timm, Bad Nauheim, 1951

"General comments. The current, provisional flag shows a white E on a green background with elongated horizontal bars. The colour green is its defining feature."

DE „Allgemeine Bemerkungen. Die bisherige, vorläufige Flagge zeigt auf grünem Grunde ein weißes E mit langgezogenen Querbalken. Ihr hervorstehendes Merkmal ist die grüne Farbe."

FR « Remarques générales. L'ancien drapeau temporaire montre un E blanc avec une longue barre transversale sur fond vert. Sa caractéristique la plus marquante est sa couleur verte. »

Walther Timm, Bad Nauheim, 1951

"To my knowledge, the simple combination of green and white without additional elements has not yet been implemented by any recognised state. Furthermore, it is a rather tasteful combination of colours. I would therefore recommend keeping it."

DE „Die Zusammenstellung Grün-Weiß ohne weitere Zutaten wird meines Wissens bisher von keinem anerkannten Staate geführt. Sie stellt auch eine geschmackvolle Farbenzusammenstellung dar. Es empfiehlt sich daher, sie beizubehalten."

FR « Autant que je sache, l'association de vert et de blanc sans autres ingrédients n'a encore été utilisée par aucun État reconnu. Elle constitue aussi une combinaison de couleurs de bon goût. Il est donc conseillé de la conserver. »

Walther Timm, Bad Nauheim, 1951

"Draft no. 3 clearly represents a progression from the current, provisional European flag. It features two narrow white stripes on a green background, whose position and width correspond to the horizontal stripes left over from the white rectangle in draft no. 2 after the insertion of the green rectangle."

DE „Der Entwurf Nr. 3 stellt eindrucksmäßig eine Fortentwicklung der bisherigen, vorläufigen Europaflagge dar. Er zeigt auf grünem Grunde zwei schmale weiße Streifen, die in Lage und Breite den nach Einfügung des grünen Rechteckes verbleibenden Längsstreifen des weißen Rechtecks in Entwurf Nr. 2 entsprechen."

FR « Le projet n° 3 représente de manière impressionnante une évolution de l'ancien drapeau européen provisoire. Il présente deux bandes blanches étroites sur fond vert, dont la position et la largeur sont les bandes longitudinales du rectangle blanc du projet n° 2 après l'insertion du rectangle vert restant. »

Walther Timm, Bad Nauheim, 1951

"I am a veteran of the First World War. In May 1915, I was seriously wounded as an ensign in a Prussian infantry regiment. I lost my eyesight as well as my right hand. It was for this personal reason that I became a supporter of the European Movement, with the hope that the age-old Franco-German conflict would finally be buried."

DE „Ich bin Teilnehmer des ersten Weltkrieges. Als Fähnrich in einem preußischen Infanterie-Regiment wurde ich im Mai 1915 schwer verwundet. Ich verlor das Augenlicht und die rechte Hand. Aus diesem persönlichen Grunde bin ich zu einem Anhänger der Europabewegung geworden, damit der Jahrhunderte alte deutsch-französische Konflikt endgültig begraben werde."

FR « J'ai participé à la Première Guerre mondiale. En tant qu'aspirant dans un régiment d'infanterie prussienne, j'ai été grièvement blessé en mai 1915. J'ai perdu la vue et ma main droite. Pour cette raison personnelle, je suis devenu un partisan du mouvement européen pour que le conflit franco-allemand vieux de plusieurs siècles puisse enfin être enterré. »

unidentified

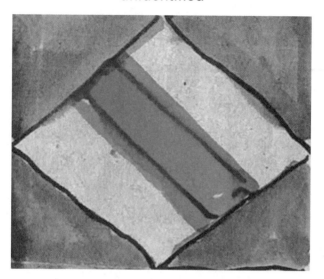

unidentified

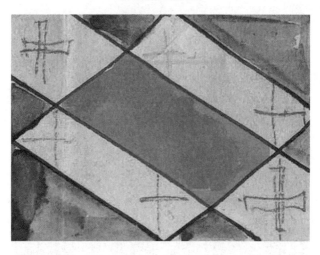

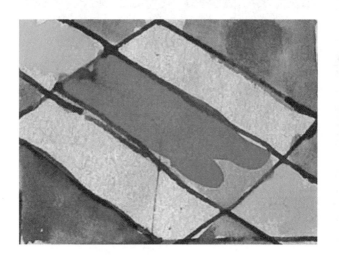

Wolfram Neue, Bad Ems, 1951

"I hereby take the liberty of presenting you with some colourful drafts for a European flag."

DE „Hierdurch erlaube ich mir, Ihnen einige farbige Entwürfe für eine Europaflagge vorzulegen."

FR « Par la présente, je me permets de vous présenter quelques projets en couleur pour un drapeau européen. »

Wolfram Neue, Bad Ems, 1951

"Since I am doing this of my own volition, I do not lay claim to any fee."

DE „Da ich dieses ohne Aufforderung dazu tue, habe ich keinerlei Honorar-Ansprüche."

FR « Puisque je fais cela sans qu'on me le demande, je ne peux prétendre à des honoraires. »

Wolfram Neue, Bad Ems, 1951

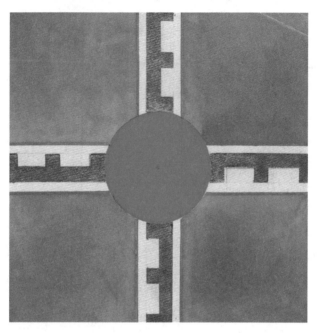

"But I would be delighted if one of the drafts were to meet with the approval of the Council of Europe and possibly be implemented in the future."

DE „Es würde mich aber freuen, wenn einer der Entwürfe das Gefallen des Europarates finden sollte und evtl. späterhin zur Ausführung kommen sollte."

FR « Mais je serais heureux si l'un des projets devait recevoir l'approbation du Conseil de l'Europe et éventuellement être mis en œuvre plus tard. »

Wolfram Neue, Bad Ems, 1951

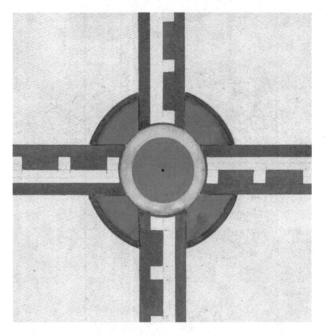

"In that event, I would be grateful to receive a small sum of money for it in due course."

DE   „In diesem Falle wäre es mir angenehm, wenn zu gegebener Zeit dann dafür ein kleiner Betrag vergütet würde."

FR   « Dans ce cas, il me serait agréable si pour cela je pouvais recevoir une petite somme en temps voulu. »

Paul F Hülse, Wiesbaden, 1951

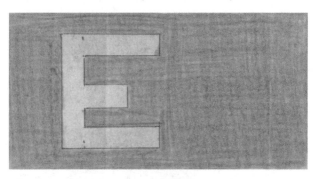

Jean Somnier, Paris, 1950

Annemarie Welker, Berlin, 1953

"The proposal is to incorporate the main colours of the national flags into the European flag, especially those that are specific to the largest nations – red, blue, white and gold."

DE „Es wird vorgeschlagen, die wichtigsten Farben der Nationalfahnen in die Europafahne zu übernehmen, insbesondere diejenigen, die gerade den größten Nationen eigen sind – Rot, Blau, Weiß und Gold."

FR « Il est proposé que les couleurs les plus importantes des drapeaux nationaux soient incluses dans le drapeau européen, en particulier celles qui sont spécifiques aux plus grandes nations – rouge, bleu, blanc et or. »

Annemarie Welker, Berlin, 1953

"In addition to the use of these colours, the following drafts for the European flag emphasise the lines of the letter E in their border design and are expected to present far fewer difficulties in terms of uniform production and general recognition."

DE „Es werden im Folgenden Entwürfe für die Europafahne dargestellt, die neben der Verwendung dieser Farben vor allen Dingen die Linienführung des Buchstabens E in der Randgestaltung erkennen lassen und der einheitlichen Fertigung und allgemeinen Anerkennung voraussichtlich weit geringere Schwierigkeiten entgegensetzen werden."

FR « Dans ce qui suit, des projets sont présentés pour le drapeau européen qui, en plus de l'utilisation de ces couleurs, révèlent surtout les lignes de la lettre E dans le dessin de la bordure et qui sont susceptibles de poser beaucoup moins de difficultés pour une production uniforme et une reconnaissance générale. »

Michel Pélot, Dijon, 1951

Michel Pélot, Dijon, 1951

unidentified

unidentified

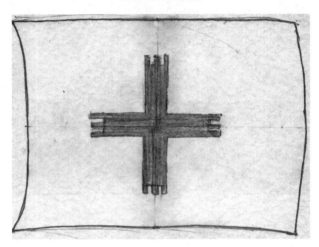

unidentified

unidentified

unidentified

unidentified

unidentified

unidentified

Mother of J. E. Dynan, Kansas City, 1950

"At the same time, it seems we have another potential Betsy Ross in the family. My mother saw my story on the flag (clipping enclosed) in the Kansas City Times, and promptly sat down and sketched her suggestion. I am likewise enclosing this with the hopes you will also put it in the flag file for committee's attention."

DE „Gleichzeitig scheint es, als hätten wir eine weitere potenzielle Betsy Ross in der Familie. Meine Mutter sah meinen Artikel über die Flagge (Ausschnitt liegt bei) in der Kansas City Times und setzte sich sofort hin und skizzierte ihren Vorschlag. Ich lege diesen ebenfalls bei in der Hoffnung, dass Sie ihn in die Akte mit den Flaggen aufnehmen, die vom Ausschuss zur Kenntnis genommen werden sollen."

FR « En même temps, il semble que nous ayons potentiellement une autre Betsy Ross dans la famille. Ma mère a vu mon article sur le drapeau (coupure jointe) dans le Kansas City Times, et s'est rapidement assise et a esquissé sa proposition. Je joins également ce document dans l'espoir que vous le placerez aussi dans le "dossier drapeau" à l'attention du comité. »

unidentified

Lex Weyer & Louis Wirion, Luxembourg, 1951

Mirko Svetkov, Novi Sad, 1951

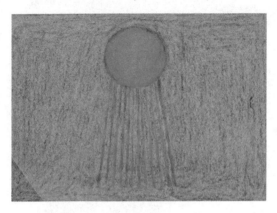

"In the above draft, the following ideas are expressed both factually and symbolically: the tribute to the Egyptian, Hellenic and Roman civilisations that preceded our civilisation; ancient Egyptian stylisation of the sun, the use of olive and orange colours so characteristic of the soil of Hellas and Rome; the communality and equality of the United States of Europe; the affinity with the flag of the United States of America: in our case, the number of rays of the sun, in theirs, the number of stars."

DE „Im obigen Entwurf kommen zum sachlichen und zum sinnbildlichen Ausdruck: die Ehrenbezeigung den unserer Zivilisation vorangegangenen ägyptischen, hellenischen und römischen Zivilisationen; altägyptische Stilisierung der Sonne, die Auswahl der für den Boden der Hellas und Roms so charakteristischen Farben der Olive und der Orange; die Gemeinschaftlichkeit und Gleichheit der Vereinigten Staaten von Europa; die Verwandschaft mit der Fahne der Vereinigten Staaten von Amerika: bei uns die Zahl der Sonnenstrahlen, dort die Zahl der Sterne."

FR « Dans le projet ci-dessus, on trouve l'expression objective et emblématique de : l'honneur des civilisations égyptienne, hellénique et romaine qui ont précédé notre civilisation ; la stylisation antique égyptienne du soleil, la sélection des couleurs olive et orange si caractéristiques du sol de Hellas et de Rome ; l'identité commune et l'égalité des États-Unis d'Europe ; la parenté avec le drapeau des États-Unis d'Amérique ; chez nous le nombre de rayons de soleil, chez eux le nombre d'étoiles. »

Erich Müller, Wiesbaden, 1953

unidentified

G. A. Bornemann, Málaga, 1952

"The Swiss flag forms the centrepiece, since Switzerland, with its location in the centre of Europe and consistent neutrality, has for many years realised the peaceful coexistence of European people of different origins and languages within its own borders."

DE „Das Mittelstück wird von der Schweizer Flagge gebildet, da die Schweiz im Zentrum Europas liegend und stets neutral, in ihren Grenzen das friedliche Zusammenleben europäischer Menschen verschiedener Abstammung und Sprache seit langem schon verwirklicht hat."

FR « La partie centrale est constituée du drapeau suisse, car la Suisse, située au centre de l'Europe et toujours neutre, a depuis longtemps réalisé la coexistence pacifique de peuples européens d'origines et de langues différentes à l'intérieur de ses frontières. »

Gambin Gaetano, Venegono Superiore, 1955

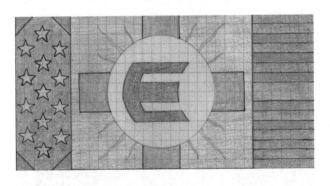

Gambin Gaetano, Venegono Superiore, 1955

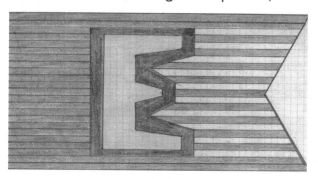

Gambin Gaetano, Venegono Superiore, 1955

unidentified

unidentified

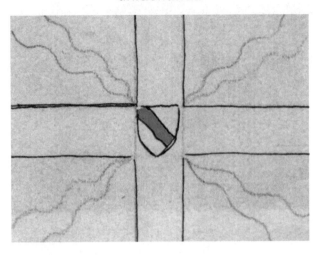

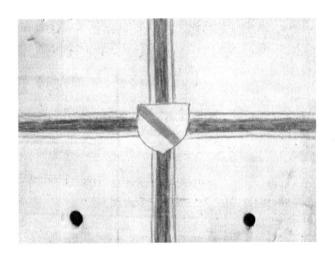

unidentified

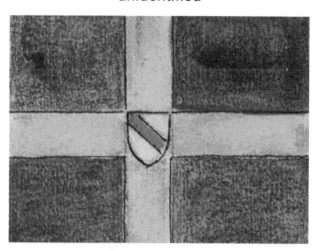

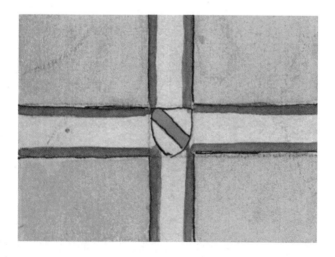

unidentified

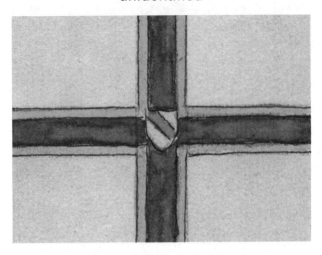

unidentified

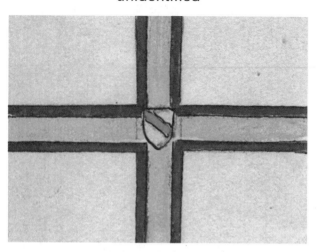

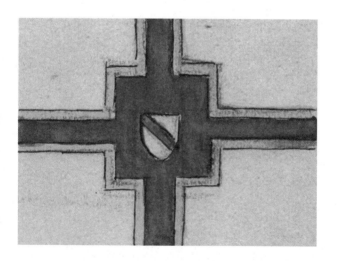

unidentified

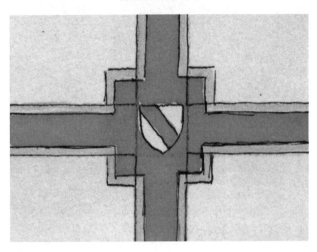

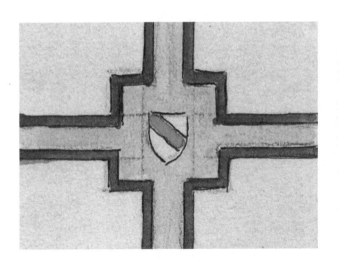

unidentified

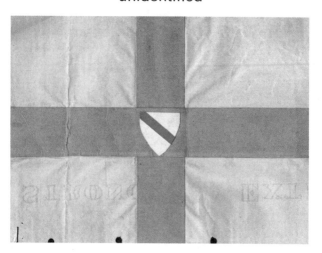

unidentified

J. E. Dynan, Paris, 1950

J. E. Dynan, Paris, 1950

Alvin Mondon, Bad Godesberg, 1950

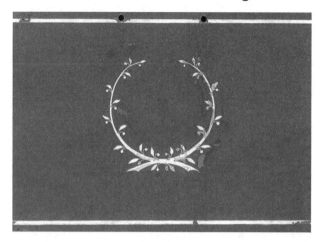

"Dear Secretary General,"

Alvin Mondon, Bad Godesberg, 1950

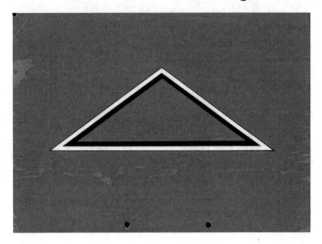

"The attached sketches illustrate the meaningful interplay of different arrangements. I consider my suggestions to be suitable for discussion and for potential selection."

DE „mit beiliegenden Skizzen, die nur ein sinnvolles Wechselspiel verschiedener Anordnungen zeigen, halte ich meine Vorschläge für diskutabel und wählbar."

FR « avec les esquisses ci-jointes, qui ne montrent qu'une alternance judicieuse de différents arrangements, je considère mes propositions comme intéressantes et éligibles. »

Alvin Mondon, Bad Godesberg, 1950

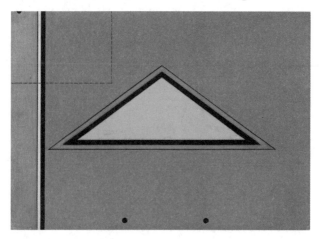

"The enemy should be confronted with a special cultural symbol, preferably the cultural triangle, or the heraldic fleur-de-lis – both could only ever be appropriate for Europe."

DE „Grundsätzlich möchte dem Gegner ein besonderes Kulturzeichen, bestens das Kulturdreieck entgegengestellt werden, desgl. die in Wappen heraldisch sprechende Lilie – beide sind nur für Europa zuständig."

FR « Fondamentalement l'adversaire aimerait s'opposer à un symbole culturel particulier, au mieux le triangle culturel, ainsi que le lys héraldique – tous deux sont représentatifs de l'Europe uniquement. »

Alvin Mondon, Bad Godesberg, 1950

"From a heraldic point of view, the signs are placed to share their centre of gravity with that of the flag – appearing correctly when seen from either side, impossible to misinterpret – allowing them to be adopted as symbols of the institutions of peace and war."

DE „Heraldisch liegen die Zeichen im gemeinsamen Schwerpunkt zur Flagge – beidseitig richtig, nicht verkennbar – und können als Symbole der Friedens- u. Kriegseinrichtungen übernommen werden."

FR « De manière héraldique, les signes sont placés en commun sur le centre de gravité du drapeau – ils se reconnaissent parfaitement et sans ambiguïté quel que soit le côté – et peuvent ainsi se lire tels les symboles des institutions garantes de la paix ou de la guerre. »

Alvin Mondon, Bad Godesberg, 1950

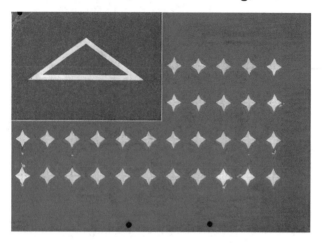

"Two star banners indicate the connection with the U.S.A.;"

Alvin Mondon, Bad Godesberg, 1950

"The yellow ones representing the assumed number of member states and the white ones the appeal."

DE   „Die gelben deuten die angenommene Zahl der zugehörigen Staaten und die weißen die Aufforderung an."

FR   « Les jaunes indiquent le nombre estimé d'États membres acceptés et associés et les blancs la demande. »

Alvin Mondon, Bad Godesberg, 1950

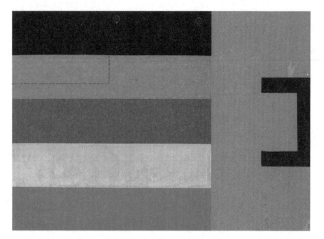

"The striped banner unites North, South, West, East and Central states with the E in what is known as the church colour."

DE   „Das Streifenbanner vereint Nord-, Süd-, West-, Ost- und Mittelstaaten mit dem E in sogenannter kirchlicher Farbe."

FR   « La bannière à rayures unit les États du nord, du sud, de l'ouest, de l'est et du centre avec le E dans la dite " couleur de l'église ". »

76

Alvin Mondon, Bad Godesberg, 1950

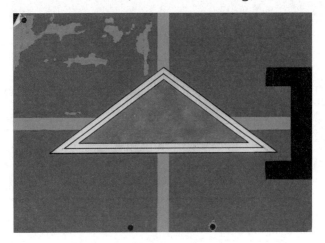

"Please allow me, dear Secretary General, to make the following remark:"

DE   „Gestatten Sie, sehr geehrter Herr Generalsekretär, folgenden Hinweis:"

FR   « Permettez, cher Monsieur le Secrétaire général, les indications suivantes : »

Alvin Mondon, Bad Godesberg, 1950

"If you accept my sketches for consideration, please indicate that you do not intend to strictly adhere to the use of colours and motifs, but rather to consider them interchangeable."

DE „Bitte geben Sie bei Annahme meiner Skizzen zur Beratung bekannt, sich nicht streng an die Wirkung der Farben und Motive halten zu wollen, sondern selbe gedanklich auszutauschen."

FR « Si vous acceptez de prendre mes esquisses en considération, veuillez s'il vous plaît transmettre de ne pas s'attacher strictement à l'effet des couleurs et des motifs, mais plutôt à ce qu'ils représentent mentalement. »

Alvin Mondon, Bad Godesberg, 1950

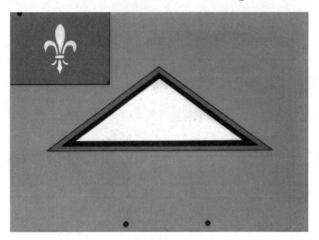

"They have a strong influence on the decision-making process, and their specification and implementation should be entrusted to a trained expert."

DE „Sie beeinflussen sehr die entscheidende Meinung und müssten in der Festlegung und auch in der Anwendung dem geschulten Fachmanne zugesprochen werden."

FR « Ils influencent grandement la prise de décision, et leurs spécifications comme leur application devraient être réservées à un expert avéré. »

Alvin Mondon, Bad Godesberg, 1950

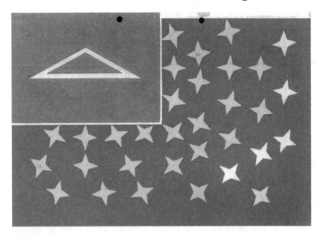

"In the hope of having served you, I look forward to your highly esteemed opinion."

DE   „In der Erwartung, Ihnen gedient zu haben, stehe ich Ihrer sehr geschätzten Stellungnahme gern entgegen."

FR   « En espérant vous avoir servi, j'attends avec impatience votre avis très estimé. »

Alvin Mondon, Bad Godesberg, 1950

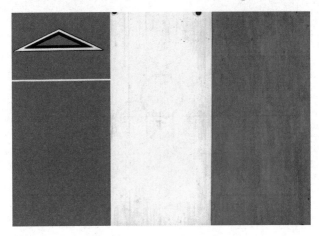

"Respectfully yours, Alvin Mondon"

DE   „Mit dem Ausdruck meiner vor-
züglichen Hochachtung, Alvin Mondon"   FR   « Avec l'expression de mes sentiments respecteux, Alvin Mondon »

81

J. P. van der Drift, Den Haag, 1954

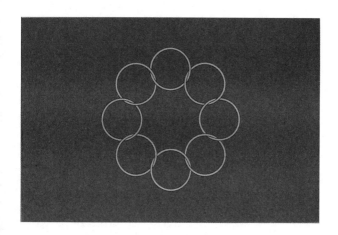

Hans Klink, Bolzano, 1951

"blue background (cornflower blue) / golden chain (possibly as many links as states) / white sword with a Chi Rho symbol / at the top of the corner each state can add its own emblem."

DE „blauer Grund (kornblumblau) / goldene kette (eventuell so viele Glieder als Staaten) / weißes Schwert mit Paxzeichen / oben im Eck kann jeder Staat dann das eigene Hoheitszeichen anbringen."

FR « Fond bleu (bleu bleuet) / chaîne dorée (éventuellement autant de maillons que d'États) / épée blanche avec signe Pax / chaque État peut ensuite placer son propre emblème national en haut dans le coin. »

unidentified

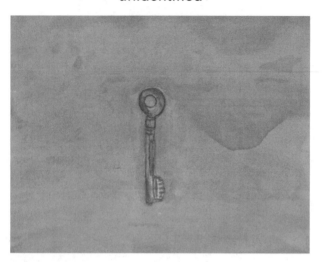

unidentified

unidentified

unidentified

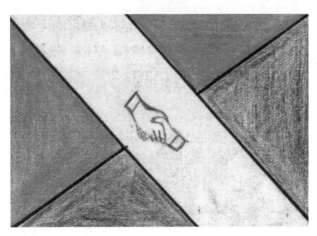

unidentified

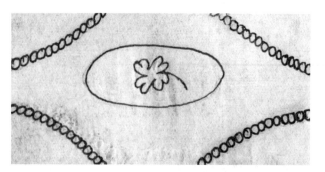

P. C. Heiser, Den Haag, 1951

"The star of the European flag is white as was the five-pointed star, used by the Allied Forces when fighting for the liberation of Western Europe from Nazi-suppression. After winning the war, now peace must be won under the same emblem."

DE „Der Stern der Europaflagge ist weiß, so, wie der fünfzackige Stern, unter dem die alliierten Streitkräfte für die Befreiung Westeuropas von den Nazis kämpften. Nachdem der Krieg gewonnen wurde, soll nun Frieden unter demselben Emblem einkehren."

FR « L'étoile du drapeau européen est blanche, comme l'étoile à cinq branches utilisée par les forces alliées lors du combat contre les Nazis pour la libération de l'Europe occidentale. Après avoir remporté la guerre, la paix doit maintenant être gagnée sous le même emblème. »

Th. Roß, Bad Sooden-Allendorf, 1950

"Here is my proposal based on the U.S.A.
The Asians can always opt for yellow stripes
later on."

DE   „Hier ist mein Vorschlag unter
Anlehnung an die USA. Die Asiaten
können ja dann später gelbe Streifen
nehmen."

FR   « Voici ma proposition basée
sur les USA. Les Asiatiques pourront
toujours prendre des bandes jaunes plus
tard. »

Robert Poucher, Paris, 1939

"They reproached me for the American appearance, or rather the bearing, of my "banner": its colours are however quite the opposite and therefore very different - and let me repeat once again that we should be grateful to the USA for what they did for us. Without their intervention, we would not have to decide on a federal banner today. One would be imposed upon us, and we certainly would not find it to our taste."

DE „Man wirft mir das amerikanische Erscheinungsbild meiner Flagge vor, oder eher ihre Tendenz: Jedoch sind ihre Farben das genaue Gegenteil und deshalb ganz anders und ich wiederhole noch einmal, dass wir den USA dankbar sein sollten für das, was sie für uns getan haben. Ohne ihr Eingreifen müssten wir uns heute nicht für eine föderale Flagge entscheiden. Man hätte uns eine auferlegt und sie wäre mit Sicherheit nicht nach unserem Geschmack gewesen."

FR « On m'a repproché l'aspect ou plutôt l'allure américaine de ma "bannière" ; les couleurs en sont pourtant nettement inverses donc différentes et je répète encore, qu'on peut être reconnaissant aux USA de ce qu'ils ont fait pour nous. Sans leur intervention, nous n'aurions pas à choisir une bannière fédérale aujourd'hui. On se serait chargé de nous en imposer une, et certes pas de notre goût. »

Werner S. Wulfing, Feldkirch, 1949

"This flag may give shape to the advent of a united Europe and of the United States of Europe."

DE   „Diese Flagge stellt vielleicht die Geburtsstunde eines vereinten Europas und auch der Vereinigten Staaten von Europa dar."

FR   « Ce drapeau sonne peut-être l'heure de naissance d'une Europe unie ainsi que des États-Unis d'Europe. »

Salvador de Madariaga, Oxford, 1952

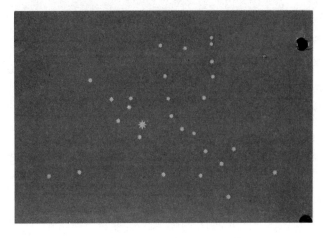

"It should both express the unity and the variety of the continent. On a blue background, the European nations that were fully souvereign in 1938 will be represented each by a golden star on the spot occupied by its capital city on the map. Strasbourg will also be represented by a slightly bigger golden star."

DE „Sie sollte sowohl die Einheit als auch die Vielfalt des Kontinents zum Ausdruck bringen. Auf blauem Hintergrund werden die europäischen Nationen, die 1938 völlig souverän waren, jeweils durch einen goldenen Stern an der Stelle, an der ihre Hauptstadt auf der Karte liegt, dargestellt. Straßburg wird durch einen etwas größeren goldenen Stern ebenfalls vertreten sein."

FR « Le drapeau doit exprimer à la fois l'unité et la variété du continent. Sur un fond bleu, les nations européennes qui étaient pleinement souveraines en 1938 seront représentées chacune par une étoile dorée à l'endroit occupé par sa capitale sur la carte. Strasbourg sera également représentée par une étoile dorée légérement plus grande. »

Joseph Oberson-Bagnolet, Bordeaux, 1952

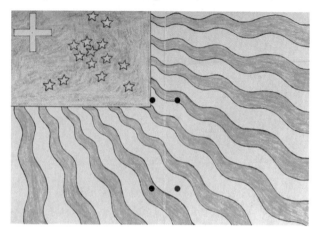

"Argent with ten wavy vert rays issuing from the charged azure canton in the dexter corner of the chief, with silver crosslet and as many five-rayed golden stars as there are member States, placed as if on a geographical map where the capitals of those States are."

DE   „Auf silbernem Grund zehn wellenförmige grüne Linkssparren ausgehend vom Gösch als ausgebrochenes Freiviertel, mit silbernem Kreuzchen und so vielen fünfzackigen goldenen Sternen wie Mitgliedsstaaten, verteilt wie auf einer geografischen Landkarte dort, wo jene Staaten liegen."

FR   « D'argent à dix rayons ondés de sinoples et mouvant de l'angle dextre du chef, au canton d'azur chargé en chef et à dextre, d'une croisette d'argent, et d'autant d'étoiles d'or à cinq rais que de pays membres, posées, comme sur une carte géographique, aux emplacements des capitales de ces États. »

unidentified

unidentified

unidentified

unidentified

Richard Coudenhove-Kalergi, 1923

"Europe ought to have an emblem to serve as a propaganda tool in conjunction with its flag, just as the Soviet star served Bolshevism and the swastika served Hitlerism. A European emblem of this kind constitutes the center of the flag of the United States of Europe: the red cross on the golden (yellow) sun. Without colours it is a cross in a circle. This design has been found on Celtic and Germanic monuments as a pre-Christian symbol of world harmony."

DE „Europa sollte ein Emblem haben, um in Verbindung mit seiner Flagge als Propagandainstrument zu dienen – so, wie der Sowjetstern dem Bolschewismus und das Hakenkreuz dem Hitlerismus. Ein solches Europa-Emblem bildet das Zentrum der Flagge der Vereinigten Staaten von Europa: das rote Kreuz auf der goldenen (gelben) Sonne. Ohne Farben ist es ein Kreuz in einem Kreis. Dieses Muster wurde als vorchristliches Symbol der Weltharmonie auf den keltischen und germanischen Denkmälern gefunden."

FR « L'Europe devrait avoir un emblème qui servirait, conjointement à son drapeau, d'outil de propagande, comme l'étoile rouge servait le bolchévisme et la croix gammée l'hitlérisme. Un emblème européen de ce type constitue le centre du drapeau des États-Unis d'Europe : la croix rouge sur le soleil d'or (jaune). Sans couleurs, il s'agit d'une croix dans un cercle. Ce motif a été découvert sur des monuments celtiques et germaniques comme symbole préchrétien de l'harmonie du monde. »

Charles Mangeney, Luxembourg, 1951

"The star could also be replaced by a sun."

DE   „Der Stern könnte durch eine Sonne ausgetauscht werden."   FR   « L'étoile pourrait également être remplacée par un soleil. »

Lex Weyer, Luxembourg, 1951

Adolf Lorder

Adolf Lorder

unidentified

unidentified

unidentified

unidentified

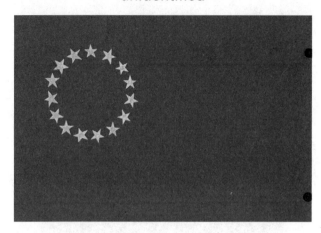

unidentified

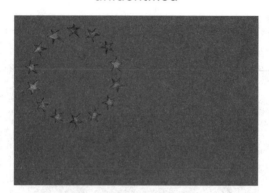

unidentified

Hanno F. Konopath, Hamburg, 1952

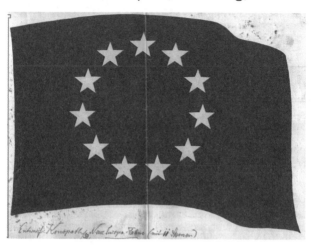

"According to my letter to you dated October 7, 1953, of which I enclose a copy, it is clear that I showed Mr. Spaak the first drafts of the golden circle of stars as early as 1951, as well as Mr. Sandys, Mr. Radoux, Mr. Friedender, Mr. Leverkusen and many others."

DE „Aus meinem Brief vom 7. Oktober 1953 an Sie, von dem ich eine Abschrift beifüge, geht klar hervor, dass ich bereits im Jahre 1951 Herrn Spaak die ersten Entwürfe des goldenen Sternenkranzes gezeigt habe, ebenso Herrn Sandys, Herrn Radoux, Herrn Friedender, Herrn Leverkusen und vielen anderen."

FR « Dans ma lettre du 7 octobre 1953 que je vous ai adressée et dont je joins une copie, il est clair que j'ai dès 1951 montré à M. Spaak les premières esquisses de la couronne d'étoiles dorées, ainsi qu'à M. Sandys, M. Radoux, M. Friedender, M. Leverkusen et d'autres encore. »

Hanno F. Konopath, Hamburg, 1952

"In addition, I found in my journal how a great number of people showed an interest in the new European flag, namely in 1951, 1952 and 1953. It is therefore impossible that it was only the emergence of the Saar question (1955) that led to the solution of the wreath of stars on a blue background. All of this is absolutely definitive in terms of time and can be proven beyond doubt by a great many prominent witnesses and press clippings."

DE „Ich habe ferner aus meinen Tagebüchern festgestellt, wie zahlreiche Personen sich für die neue Europafahne interessiert haben, und zwar 1951, 1952 und 1953. Es ist also nicht so, dass erst nach dem Auftauchen der Saarfrage (1955) die Lösung des Sternenkranzes auf blauem Grunde vorgelegt worden wäre. Das Alles steht zeitlich absolut fest und kann durch sehr viele prominente Zeugen und durch Presseausschnitte unzweifelhaft bewiesen werden."

FR « J'ai en outre retrouvé dans mon journal le nombre élevé de personnes qui ont manifesté de l'intérêt pour le nouveau drapeau européen, à savoir en 1951, 1952 et 1953. Il n'est donc pas vrai que la solution de la couronne d'étoiles sur fond bleu ait été décidée uniquement après l'apparition de la question de la Sarre (1955). Tout cela est absolument clair chronologiquement et peut être prouvé sans aucun doute par un grand nombre de témoins éminents et de coupures de presse. »

Hanno F. Konopath, Hamburg, 1952

"In my letter dated October 7, 1953, I had written to you that I felt I was the author of the new European flag, and no one has ever denied that to date."

DE „In meinem Brief vom 7. Oktober 1953 hatte ich Ihnen geschrieben, dass ich mich als Autor der neuen Europafahne fühle, und das hat mir auch bisher niemand bestritten."

FR « Dans ma lettre du 7 octobre 1953, je vous avais écrit que je me sentais comme l'auteur du nouveau drapeau européen, et personne ne l'a contredit jusqu'à présent. »

Hanno F. Konopath, Hamburg, 1952

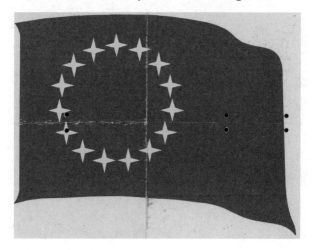

"But now comes your essay in the journal 'Terre d'Europe', in which I am only mentioned as the organiser of a kind of survey, and in any case not as the creator of the design of the golden wreath of stars on a blue background."

DE „Nun aber kommt Ihr Aufsatz in der Revue ‚Terre d'Europe', in dem von mir lediglich als Veranstalter einer Art Umfrage die Rede ist, jedenfalls nicht als Schöpfer des Entwurfes des Goldenen Sternenkranzes auf blauem Grunde."

FR « Mais voilà que paraît maintenant votre contribution dans la revue " Terre d'Europe ", dans laquelle je ne suis désigné que comme l'organisateur d'une sorte de sondage, et pas en tant que créateur du projet de la couronne d'étoiles d'or sur fond bleu. »

Hanno F. Konopath, Hamburg, 1952

"This raises the question: Does anyone besides me claim to be the creator of this design? If so, who is it? And when did he submit the draft, and how can he prove it?"

DE   „Es erhebt sich also die Frage: Macht außer mir noch jemand den Anspruch geltend, Schöpfer dieses Entwurfes zu sein? Wenn ja, wer ist es? Und wann hat er den Entwurf vorgelegt, und wie kann er es beweisen?"

FR   « La question se pose donc : est-ce que quelqu'un d'autre que moi prétend être le créateur de ce dessin ? Si oui, qui est-ce ? et quand a-t-il présenté le projet et comment peut-il le prouver ? »

Hanno F. Konopath, Hamburg, 1952

"In 1953 I wrote to you that I 'trustingly leave the matter in your hands.' Since nothing followed, I thought it fair to assume that, for your part, you recognised that I was the author of the design, on the basis of the numerous documents sent to you."

DE „1953 habe ich Ihnen geschrieben, dass ich ‚die Sache vertrauensvoll in Ihre Hände lege.' – Da darauf nichts erfolgte, konnte ich annehmen und habe ich angenommen, dass Ihrerseits die Tatsache meiner Vaterschaft auf Grund der Ihnen übersandten zahlreichen Unterlagen anerkannt ist."

FR « En 1953, je vous ai écrit que " je vous confiais l'affaire en toute confiance ". Puisque rien n'a suivi, j'ai donc pu supposer et je considère que le fait de ma paternité est reconnu de votre part, sur la base des nombreux documents qui vous ont été adressés. »

Hanno F. Konopath, Hamburg, 1952

"After all, I have been working on this wonderful task for many years, I came up with this artistic idea, which I continue to take great pleasure in, as does everyone I talk to about it, and now I would like this copyright to be recognised and protected just like any other."

DE „Schließlich habe ich jahrelang an dieser schönen Aufgabe gearbeitet, habe diese künstlerische Idee gehabt, an der ich immer wieder meine Freude habe, wie Sie auch und jeder, mit dem ich darüber spreche, und möchte nun, dass dieses Urheberrecht, wie jedes andere auch, anerkannt und geschützt wird."

FR « Après tout, j'ai travaillé sur cette belle tâche pendant des années, j'ai eu cette idée artistique, que j'apprécie toujours, tout comme vous et tous ceux à qui j'en parle, et maintenant je voudrais que ce droit d'auteur, comme tous les autres également, soit reconnu et protégé. »

Hanno F. Konopath, Hamburg, 1952

"I have absolute confidence that the matter will be settled in a fair manner."

DE   „Ich habe das absolute Vertrauen, dass die Sache in fairer Weise geregelt wird."

FR   « J'ai la confiance absolue que les choses seront traitées équitablement. »

Arsène Heitz, Strasbourg

Arsène Heitz, Strasbourg, 1951

"I have the honour of presenting you with a design for a European flag with a green background matching the colour of Charlemagne's flag, which was presented to him by Pope Leo III at the coronation in Rome on December 25, 800."

DE „Ich habe die Ehre, Ihnen einen Entwurf für die Europaflagge zu präsentieren mit grünem Hintergrund, der Farbe der Flagge Karls des Großen, die ihm von Papst Leo III. zur Krönung in Rom am 25. Dezember 800 übergeben wurde."

FR « J'ai l'honneur de vous soumettre un projet de drapeau européen, dont le fond est vert, couleur de l'étendard de Charlemagne, qui lui a été offert par le Pape Léon III, lors du couronnement, le 25 décembre en l'An 800 à Rome. »

Arsène Heitz, Strasbourg, 1951

"The red cross represents the blood that European soldiers have shed throughout the centuries. The double yellow cross, which accompanies the red cross, is the emblem of the Christian world and the colour of the Vatican."

DE „Das rote Kreuz stellt das Blut dar, das europäische Soldaten über die Jahrhunderte vergossen haben. Das doppelte gelbe Kreuz, welches das rote Kreuz umgibt, ist das Emblem des Christentums und die Farbe des Vatikans."

FR « La croix rouge représente le sang répandu par les guerriers européens, depuis des siècles. La double croix jaune accompagnant la croix rouge est l'emblème du monde chrétien, et la couleur du Vatican. »

Arsène Heitz, Strasbourg, 1951

"Each country that is a member of the Council of Europe has the option of placing its national flag in the center of the red cross, either in the form of a coat of arms or a small flag."

DE „Jedes Land, welches Mitglied des Europarats ist, hat die Möglichkeit, die eigene Nationalflagge in der Mitte des roten Kreuzes zu platzieren, entweder als Wappen oder als kleine Flagge."

FR « Chaque pays membre du Conseil de l'Europe aura le choix d'ajouter au centre de la croix rouge, son pavillon national, sous forme de blason ou petit drapeau. »

Arsène Heitz, Strasbourg, 1952

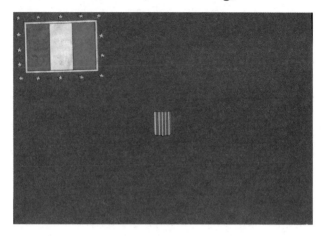

"Since it is difficult to do away with national ensigns overnight, each state will find its respective place in the European flag, at least as a transitional measure."

DE   „Da es schwierig ist, die Nationalflaggen von einem Tag auf den anderen abzuschaffen oder zu ignorieren, wird jeder Staat seinen jeweiligen Platz in der europäischen Flagge wiederfinden, zumindest übergangsweise."

FR   « Comme il est difficile de supprimer ou d'ignorer d'un jour à l'autre les pavillons nationaux, chaque États trouvera sa place respective dans le drapeau européen, au moins à titre transitoire. »

Arsène Heitz, Strasbourg, 1952

Arsène Heitz, Strasbourg, 1952

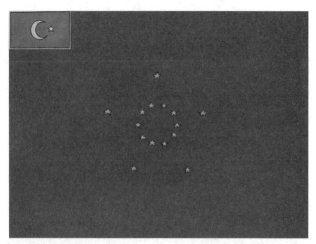

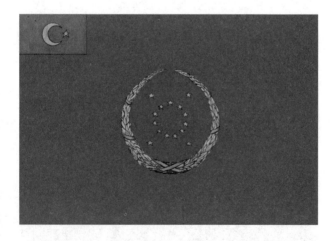

Arsène Heitz, Strasbourg, 1952

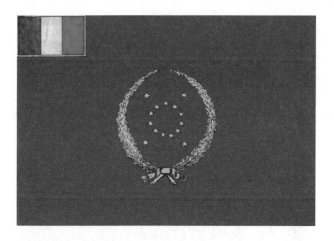

Arsène Heitz, Strasbourg, 1952

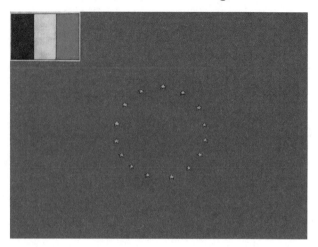

126

Arsène Heitz, Strasbourg, 1952

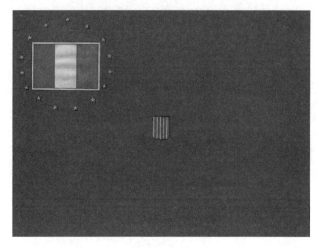

Arsène Heitz, Strasbourg, 1952

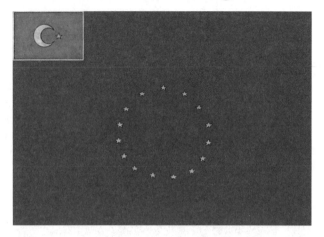

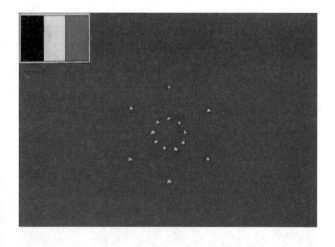

Arsène Heitz, Strasbourg, 1954

"Azure with a closed crown of oak and olive tree leaves, in the fess point a big five-branched star representing all the States composing the Council of Europe, surrounded by fourteen little golden stars. Symbol: the closed golden crown, on the azure encircling the stars, represents union."

DE „Auf azurblauem Grund eine goldene Krone umschlossen von Eichen- und Olivenblättern, in der Mitte ein gro-ßer fünfzackiger Stern als Zeichen für die Gemeinschaft aller Staaten des Europa-rates, umgeben von vierzehn kleinen goldenen Sternen. Das Symbol: Die geschlossene goldene Krone auf azur-blauem Grund und umkreist von Sternen ist das Zeichen der Vereinigung."

FR « D'azur à une couronne d'or fermée à feuilles de chêne et d'olivier, dans l'abîme une grande étoile d'or à cinq branches représentant l'ensemble des États du Conseil de l'Europe, entou-rée de quatorze petites étoiles d'or. Symbole : la couronne d'or fermée, sur l'azur ceinturant les étoiles, est signe d'union. »

Arsène Heitz, Strasbourg, 1953

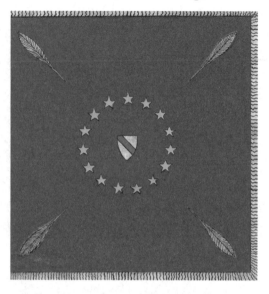

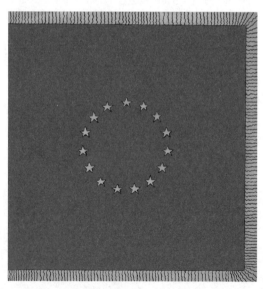

Arsène Heitz, Strasbourg, 1953

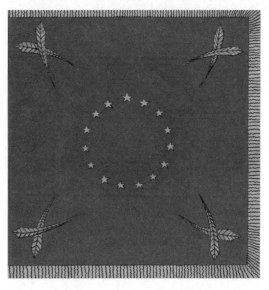

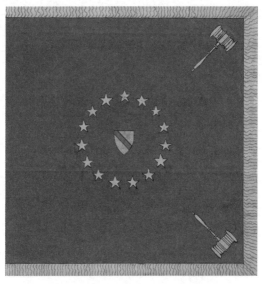

Arsène Heitz, Strasbourg, 1953

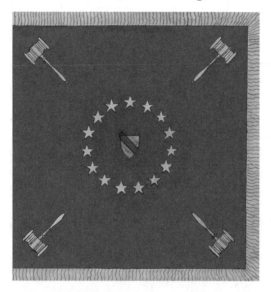

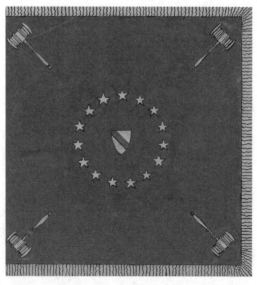

Arsène Heitz, Strasbourg

"Azure with a circle of fourteen five-branched golden stars, whose points do not touch. In the fess point, the fifth star stands for all the States composing the Council of Europe."

DE „Auf azurblauem Grund ein Kreis von vierzehn fünfzackigen goldenen Sternen, deren Spitzen sich nicht berühren. Der fünfzehnte Stern in der Mitte steht für die Gemeinschaft der Staaten des Europarats."

FR « D'azur à un cercle de quatorze étoiles d'or à cinq branches, dont les pointes ne se touchent pas. Dans l'abîme, la quinzième étoile représente l'ensemble des États du Conseil de l'Europe. »

Arsène Heitz, Strasbourg, 1954

Arsène Heitz, Strasbourg, 1954

Arsène Heitz, Strasbourg, 1955

Arsène Heitz, Strasbourg, 1955

Arsène Heitz, Strasbourg, 1954

Arsène Heitz, Strasbourg, 1954

NEW NEW ORDER

13 colonies. 13 colonies and 13 stars in a circle on blue cloth, the blue of the sky, on the first flag of the United States of America. A flag to bring people together around a symbol, to bring territories to heel. 13, the number of good fortune. The number of a will fulfilled, of independence, of a break with history. A flag for the invention of liberty.

A flag for a new world, for outcast Europeans, a long journey, and always hope. The hope of blue skies, of female eyes.

And the most beautiful inventions are those imagined and woven by women, with patience and in harmony with their times, with a pragmatic sense of nature. In 1776, Betsy Ross gave us a piece of her dreams when she sewed the first flag of the USA.

12, the number of the Mission. 12 like the number of stars in the halo of the Virgin Mary. 12 like the Christians. 12 like the blood of Christ. 12 like civilization. 12 like the Atlantic triangular slave trade. 1+2. The trinity. 12 like the 327 Indian Reservations in the USA.

12 stars on your EU flag.

Blessed is he who has no home; he sees it still in his dreams, wrote Hannah Arendt in an almost anti-romantic poem in 1946. Arendt, who never wished for a home, longed for a feeling of security, something that cannot in any way be compared with the strange German word *Heimat.* She longed for the feeling of feelings, far removed from any territory. Because territories are for spoilt children or lost Protestants with inferiority complexes in pursuit of an identity. Those who are free can see the dictatorship of identities.

As a woman, I have no country. As a woman I want no country. As a woman my country is the whole world, replied Virginia Woolf as an echo to Hannah Arendt in 1938. Together, they bury the idea of belonging and drill holes through time. Women without a home and without a country, universal women with no prescribed identity. Human beings who need no flags.

1949 to 1955, the Council of Europe in Strasbourg: men with small drawings and big flags in search of forgiveness. The crown of twelve gold stars on an azure ground was selected by the Council of Europe on 8 December 1955, the feast day of the Immaculate Conception of Mary, woman of purity and apocalypse. The flag was designed by the Catholic Arsène Heitz or by the good Jew Paul M.G. Lévy, who converted to Catholicism out of gratitude for having survived World War II.

All these children's drawings! Take a look, be brave! Leaf through the book of failed Europe. Do it for your own children. Side by side, painted for a good cause, in the name of peace, as the triumph of good over evil.

"We need adults in the room", said Christine Lagarde on 18 June 2015, as managing director of the International Monetary Fund (IMF), speaking to Eurozone finance ministers during the Greek sovereign debt crisis. What is the Greek tragedy worth compared with the Erasmus Programme? Nothing. Erasmus continues to serve social reproduction,[1] even if educated middle-class youth were already travelling around Europe long before the Programme was invented.

"We must all send out positive energy to counter-act all these negative tendencies. The European pulse must be felt everywhere!" Instead of making political demands on the EU, the *Pulse of Europe* club propagates a positive mood towards the EU. "In their rejection of EU critics with populist and nationalist attitudes, however, the demonstrators overlook those who are voicing legitimate criticism of the EU, simply counting them among their enemies," one of my students, herself a pro-EU activist, wrote to me, disappointed.[2] Blue hoodies printed with yellow stars. Europe fan clubs and marketing symbols as a substitute for EU politics: the de-politicization of Europe's youth is promoted by the EU itself. And always this perverse switching of the terms *EU* and *Europe*. Today, former German vice-chancellor Philipp Rösler would say: Europe is the coolest country in the world.

Unfortunately, young people in Germany will not have a chance to watch Costa-Gavras' film *Adults in the Room* (2019). It was censored, not picked up by a single German distributor, and described in the few reviews it received as "unreservedly subjective".[3] And this although Costa-Gavras toned down the historical reality: Christine Lagarde, now President of the European Central Bank, is portrayed as more conciliatory than she really is, and Angela Merkel works in the background to temper the aggressiveness of Wolfgang Schäuble.

1

See Magali Ballatore, Thierry Blöss, "L'autre réalité du programme Erasmus," in *Formation emploi-Revue française de sciences sociales* 103 (2008) and "Partir en Erasmus : et après ?" in *Spirale - Revue de recherche en* éducation 51 (2013).

2

I would like to take this opportunity to thank my students: what good fortune to have met such intelligent and curious people!

3

www.german-foreign-policy.com/news/detail/8331/ (accessed 10 July 2020).

ILLUSION AND PROPAGANDA
Translation: Solidarity and Perspective

I could carry on with Hannah Arendt and Virginia Woolf, the heroines of my youth. I could use my pen to let them converse, inventing righteous feminist and even anti-nationalist ideas. That's how I would have done it back then, when I didn't yet live in Germany. Sometimes I feel like Leni Riefenstahl in *Africa* or *The Last of The Nuba*. Like her, I study the natives. Like her, I like watching women dance. Like her, I like *men who come from another planet*. That was before, when I had not yet mixed my blood with the Germans. Back then, holes through time.

That was before certain words took on different meanings through their new usage: progressivism, populism, illiberal democracy and – democracy.

I know, it's vulgar to talk about democracy. Everyone knows the 2005 referendum in which the majority of the French people voted *against* accepting the European Constitutional Treaty. Everyone knows that the European Parliament has no power, that the European Commission makes financial and budget laws without having to present them to the national parliaments for debate. Everyone knows how and where to find magic money (as Emmanuel Macron calls it) in order to create more debt. Everyone knows that democracy is a bijou, an accessory, and that there are different interpretations of what it means. Although one must add: the EU was non-democratic from the outset. And strangely, as I get older, I demand more and more democracy from the society in which I live. But then again, I was raised in France.

Everyone knows that the European Union mocks its populations. For years, many important thinkers[4] have been showing us how the EU opposes democracy and social rights. The word *reform* is a euphemism for: no more welfare state. Today, it is poverty that is shared, not wealth. In France it will soon be the same as in Germany's civil service: no right to strike. You want humane pensions? A sit-in outside the European Commission is your only option. Voting in one's own country has become folklore.

That was before Alain Supiot, a legal scholar at the Collège de France, warned us that the ruling of Germany's Federal Constitutional Court of 5 May 2020 concerning bond purchases by the European Central Bank was a further important step towards consolidating the absolute hegemony of Germany in the European Union. And as a philosopher of law, he stressed again and again: solidarity is neither an insurance policy nor an act of charity.

That was before I read books like *Libres d'obéir* (Free To Obey)[5] by Johann Chapoutot. In his courageous text, he shows how Germany has perpetuated Nazi methods by establishing a hinterland (something Polish and Ukrainian

4
Wolfgang Streeck, François Denord, Antoine Schwartz, Andreas Wehr, Coralie Delaume, David Cayla, Frédéric Lordon, Frédéric Farah, Emmanuel Todd, les Économistes Atterrés: Thank you all.

5
Johann Chapoutot, *Libres d'obéir. Le management, du nazisme à aujourd'hui* (Paris 2020).

healthcare workers would not deny). The book is about Reinhard Höhn, the former SS-Oberführer and founder of the post-war Academy for Business Leaders in Bad Harzburg, a symptomatic figure, an appalling allegory on the desire to avenge Germany's defeat and to attempt "to sublimate it by turning one's country into an economic giant".

That was before the Special European Council of 21 July 2020 once more revealed the neoliberal dogmas of the EU. The economic recovery plan to tackle the crisis caused by the COVID-19 pandemic served as a pretext to cement the total power of the troika (European Commission, European Central Bank, IMF). Angela Merkel is our Margaret Thatcher. Hiding behind the "Frugal Four" and her most trusted partner Mark Rutte, she won her two-track game.[6] The future of indirect development aid and exploitation of the workforce is now secure until at least 2027. The other countries to the East and the South, including France, are being deprived of their rights to decide, in the spirit captured as early as the 1960s by the cabaret artist Wolfgang Neuss: "Wir schaffen es, ohne Waffen-SS" (We can do it, without the Waffen-SS).

We should also not forget the unambiguous statements by Manfred Weber, leader of the conservative European People's Party in the EU parliament: in May 2020 he was already calling for strict controls with direct EU access to the data of net recipient countries like Spain and Italy.

The struggle for life, in an azure blue sky. *God with us,* wrapped in an EU flag.

We must also realize that the *European question* is linked to "progressive" parties like the Greens or the SPD.[7] The AfD in Germany and *le Rassemblement national* in France are symptoms. They are the result of social-democratic and green politics, the result of wilful market radicalism, privatization, the dismantling of the welfare state, and the upwards redistribution of wealth.

As a *supranational* association of states, the EU is based on necessary competition between its countries. It bends to the greed of investors and government debt is the instrument by which the markets rule. This, incidentally, is a European speciality that does not exist in Japan or the United States, whose central banks are allowed to buy government bonds directly, which is prohibited here by the Treaty of Maastricht. In 2015, Jean-Claude Juncker admitted: "There can be no democratic choice against the European treaties."[8]

The federalism of the European Union does not lead to solidarity between member states. Instead, as stressed by Frédéric Farah, it is authoritarian and punitive. This has nothing to do with true federalism.

Yanis Varoufakis or Thomas Piketty are doubtlessly sad now they have understood that reforms within the system of the EU are impossible.

6
www.bloombergquint.com/politics/merkel-says-need-to-combine-aid-with-reforms-in-signal-to-rutte (accessed 31 August 2020).

7
The party that ran its 2019 European election campaign under the slogan "Europe is the answer".

8
www.lefigaro.fr/conjoncture/2015/01/28/20002-20150128ARTFIG00441-jean-claude-juncker-pas-question-de-supprimer-la-dette-grecque.php (accessed 31 August 2020)

The European elites are perfectly aware of this. Anyone wishing to work politically for democracy and social justice must declare the EU invalid and stop waiting for the Messiah who is never going to come anyway. He's already here, he's called Martin Luther.

That was before I opened a letter given to me to read by Jonas von Lenthe. In it, the Yugoslavian Mirko Cvetkov explains his idea for the European flag: a radiant sun symbolizing our civilization founded on Hellenic, Roman and Egyptian culture. It is a bitter irony to learn of the state of mind in which he submitted his flag design. The drawing is an expression of his wish for equality, community and peace. In 1951, the word was: No more war! How dramatic, when one knows how the story continued: the Yugoslavian wars, *divide et impera*, with the help of the United States, so that the republics of the former Yugoslavia belong to the EU. The Balkanization of Yugoslavia was accelerated by Germany's recognition of Slovenia and Croatia in 1992, followed by Germany's first military operation since World War II, just after Reunification. In 1999, at the Château de Rambouillet, Gerhard Schröder and Joschka Fischer decided to bomb in the name of peace:[9] *Si vis pacem, para bellum*. "The Europe of Brussels", to paraphrase Joschka Fischer in 1995, was thus the guarantor of peace. In this same spirit, official EU brochures to this day tell us that Europe protects us from war. Do these wars with their ethnic cleansing somehow not count?

We should also not forget that Europe has become a fortress, thanks to Angela Merkel who divided up the tasks after *Operation Refugee* in 2015: leaving the dirty work to Turkey *and* having refugee camps built at hotspots on the Greek islands (in turn supporting Franco-German engineering projects). Camps were then also built in Italy and later in Libya. There, the refugees are looked after by Frontex staff, the European Asylum Support Office, and other subcontractors, cash-flow from slavery.

In 2012, the European Union won the Nobel Peace Prize. This might be a conspiracy.

And one day, the Reverend Joachim Gauck came to Oradour-sur-Glane, the site of the Oradour massacre of 10 June 1944. And he said to us on 4 September 2013: *TODAY GERMANY IS A GOOD COUNTRY. IT WANTS TO BUILD EUROPE, BUT NOT TO DOMINATE IT*

How can the political scientist Claus Leggewie claim, in a lecture on Europe's climate policy, that Ursula von der Leyen and the European Commission will take a leading role on ecological issues when the history and modus operandi of the EU – always to the advantage of global players – are well known? What to do with these contradictions?

Such misunderstandings are also to be found when one makes comparative studies. Take the newspapers *Le Monde diplomatique France* and *Le Monde diplomatique Deutschland*. Serge Halimi writes with great clarity in many

9
www.cairn.info/revue-etudes-germaniques-2009-2-page-471.htm# (accessed 31 August 2020)

of his editorials: if you want ecology, you have to do without neoliberalism. In March 2019, *Le Monde diplomatique France* published *Une Union à refaire,*[10] a dossier written by opponents of the EU. That would be inconceivable in Germany, where *Le Monde diplomatique* publishes Ulrike Guérot, a Macronist and lobbyist for a *European Republic,* or Robert Menasse, who constantly calls for less Hugo Boss and more United Colors of Benetton in the EU, instead of unmasking *Germania Magna*.

We have a problem that has long ceased to be a question: speaking about the EU means having to speak about Germany. The horizon is not enough. Pan-Germanism has the colour of the sky and the stars of the American dream, the great illusion.

The historian Emmanuel Todd is not the only one who knows that the Germans secretly hate the Americans. And I don't feel sorry, neither for the goddaughter of Alfred Herrhausen, Carolin Emcke,[11] nor for *Le Monde* journalist Sylvie Kauffmann, both of whom are so full of German and French right-mindedness. We know that German generosity is always subject to conditions.

George Orwell knew this, too. But Armin Nassehi didn't get the memo in 2020 when he wrote an afterword to the first German publication of Orwell's essay "Notes on Nationalism".[12] The EU has made Europe far too decadent, thinks Orwell as he turns in his grave, you couldn't make it up! Forcing me to spew propaganda about a supposedly federal Europe and putting words into my mouth I never wanted to say, do the Germans hate the British, too? Orwell would never have wanted *Germania Magna* and he would have voted for Brexit, in the name of Britain's sovereignty and independence. How can Armin Nassehi claim the opposite in an afterword for a text written by the Socialist George Orwell in 1945?

The scandal of the EU is the destruction of the sovereignty of Europe's peoples, tearing it up under the pretext of nationalism.

In his official speeches, on the other hand, Emmanuel Macron is still selling us French and European sovereignty at the same time – apparently he has forgotten that, according to the legal definition, the sovereignty of the people is indivisible and that each people's right to self-determination is one of the pillars of international law.

It's too late. In France, everyone hates the police. In Europe, everyone hates the EU and the Germans. It would be good if the Germans knew this.

Because in Germany, being against nationalism is a matter of repression, of denial. The war strategy behind this is as follows: suppress aspirations to sovereignty in the other European countries in order to fuel German nationalism and, with this terrible paradox, bring all right-wing extremists into position.

10
www.monde-diplomatique.
fr/2019/03/GUENOLE/59606
(accessed 31 August 2020)

11
"Yes, but happiness is not the same as home," Eva Illouz replied to Carolin Emcke. Carolin Emcke and Eva Illouz im conversation, in: programme booklet for the first season of 2016/17, Schaubühne, Berlin.

12
George Orwell, *Über Nationalismus*, with an afterword by Armin Nassehi (Munich 2020).

The populations of Italy, Greece, Spain and France – which must accept at last that it belongs to the south of Europe – wish for Germany to leave the European Union and for Ursula von der Leyen to drown.

Things have become so tragic that even Emmanuel Todd has become shy. Today, he no longer speaks of Germany's responsibilities within the European Union, but about "Germany's Difference", even if we know this is Jewish humour that the natives will never understand. They prefer to watch *Unorthodox* on Netflix to see the traumatized city of Berlin presented as a city of freedom.

Frédéric Lordon said we should never have created a joint currency with Germany, the cursed nation.[13] Germany is a monster, said Émile Durkheim in 1915, a self-destructive people that suffers from a pathology of idealism. Vladimir Jankélévitch has taught us how we should translate the words of Joachim Gauck: "The twisting of contradictions has always been the speciality of German Machiavellianism."[14] If we wanted to live, we should have fought a war not against a virus but against this monster.

The curse of the Germans – this is the chimera of the European Union. The German elites are cursed and they know perfectly well that being German is a Greek tragedy, maybe worse than the decline of the Roman Empire.

The European flag is a flag for the Germans.
Its function: to escape their destiny.

THE ABILITY NOT TO BELONG

"Ich bin keine Berlinerin. All free people, wherever they may live, are citizens who struggle against

Berlin, and therefore, as a free women, I take pride in the words: Never become German."[15]

Germany, European Union, I will not carry your cross and I will never want to share it with you. I do not want to belong to this *Volksgemeinschaft,* because this society has nothing to do with Europe.

I will bow down at the grave of Émile Durkheim in Montparnasse Cemetery in Paris and comfort him. I will bring him milk and honey before he turns in his grave because he sees that the EU has become the new religion. The German lie in the name of peace, of the countries of Europe.

What is to be done? Émile Durkheim might say:
Now we need weapons.
As a woman, I say: Write love letters.
From now on, we will write nothing but love letters. We will write love letters to Carolin Emcke.

And a bridge will always take shape over the cultural rifts that divide the populations, because *Germany cannot fulfil the destiny she has marked out for herself without preventing humanity from living in freedom, and life will not submit to perpetual enslavement.*[16]

Marie Rotkopf, August 2020

13
Frédéric Farah, *Fake State* (Saint-Martin-de-Londres 2020).

14
Vladimir Jankélévitch, *L'impre-scriptible, Dans l'honneur et la dignité* (Paris 1986).

15
Freely adapted from John F. Kennedy's 1963 speech in Berlin.

16
Émile Durkheim, *L'Allemagne au-dessus de tout* (Paris 1915).

VÖLKERORDNUNG

13 Kolonien. 13 Kolonien und 13 Sterne in einem Kreis auf blauem Stoff, dem Blau des Himmels, auf der ersten Flagge der Vereinigten Staaten von Amerika. Eine Fahne, um Menschen durch ein Symbol zu verbünden, um Territorien zu bezähmen. 13, die Zahl der Chance. Die Zahl der Vollendung eines Willens und die der Unabhängigkeit, des Bruchs mit der Geschichte. Eine Flagge zur Erfindung der Freiheit.

Eine Flagge für eine neue Welt, für verstoßene Europäer, eine lange Reise, und immer die Hoffnung. Hoffnung auf einen blauen Himmel, auf weibliche Augen.

Und die schönsten Erfindungen sind die, die von Frauen imaginiert und gewebt worden sind, mit Geduld und im Einklang mit der Zeit, mit dem pragmatischen Sinn der Natur. Betsy Ross schenkte uns 1776 ein Stück von ihren Träumen, als sie die erste Fahne der USA nähte.

12, die Zahl der Mission. 12 wie die Zahl der Sterne, die das Haupt Mariens' bekränzen. 12 wie die Christen. 12 wie das Blut Jesus. 12 wie die Zivilisation. 12 wie der atlantische Dreieckshandel. 1+2. Dreifaltigkeit. 12 wie die aktuellen 327 Indianer-Reservate in den USA.

12 Sterne auf eurer EU-Flagge.

Wohl dem, der keine Heimat hat; er sieht sie noch im Traum, schrieb Hannah Arendt 1946 in einem fast antiromantischen Gedicht. Hannah Arendt, die sich nie eine Heimat wünschte, sehnte sich nach Geborgenheit, etwas, das keineswegs mit diesem merkwürdigen deutschen Wort *Heimat* zu vergleichen ist. Sie sehnte sich nach dem

Gefühl der Gefühle, meilenweit von jedem Territorium entfernt. Denn Territorien sind für verwöhnte Kinder oder verlorene Protestant*innen mit Minderwertigkeitskomplexen, die nach einer Identität streben. Wer frei ist, erkennt die Diktatur der Identitäten.

Und in Wahrheit habe ich als Frau kein Land. Als Frau will ich kein Land haben. Als Frau ist mein Land die ganze Welt, antwortete Virginia Woolf 1938 als Echo auf Hannah Arendt. Zusammen begraben sie die Idee der Zugehörigkeit und bohren Löcher in die Zeit. Frauen ohne Heimat und ohne Land, universelle Frauen ohne vorgegebene Identität. Menschen, die keine Fahnen brauchen.

1949 bis 1955, Europarat in Straßburg: Männer mit kleinen Zeichnungen und großen Flaggen auf der Suche nach Vergebung. Der Kranz aus zwölf goldenen Sternen auf azurblauem Grund wurde am 8. Dezember 1955 vom Europarat ausgewählt, dem Tag der unbefleckten Empfängnis Mariens, Frau der Reinheit und Apokalypse. Die Flagge wurde von dem Katholiken Arsène Heitz oder von dem guten Juden Paul M.G. Lévy entworfen, der aus Dank, dass er den zweiten Weltkrieg überlebt hatte, zum Katholizismus konvertierte.

All diese Kinderzeichnungen! Schauen Sie sich das an, trauen Sie sich! Blättern Sie im Buch des gescheiterten Europas. Machen Sie es für Ihre eigenen Kinder. Seite für Seite, gemalt für einen guten Zweck, im Namen des Friedens und als Triumph des Guten über das Böse.

„We need adults in the room", sagte Christine Lagarde am 18. Juni 2015, damals geschäftsführende Direktorin des Internationalen Währungsfonds (IWF), zu den Finanzministern der Euro-Zone während der griechischen Staatsschuldenkrise. Was ist die griechische Tragödie wert im Vergleich zum Erasmus-Programm? Nichts. Es dient weiterhin der gesellschaftlichen Reproduktion[1] und man sollte nicht vergessen, dass die gehobene Mittelschichtsjugend – um das Wort *Klasse* für die deutsche Leserschaft nicht zu erwähnen – auch schon vor der Erfindung des Erasmus-Programms durch Europa gereist ist.

„Lasst uns positive Energie aussenden, die den negativen Tendenzen entgegenwirkt. Der europäische Pulsschlag muss spürbar sein!" Anstatt konkrete politische Forderungen an die EU zu stellen, propagiert der Verein *Pulse of Europe* lieber eine positive Grundstimmung gegenüber der EU. „In ihrer Ablehnung von EU-Kritiker*innen mit populistischen und nationalistischen Haltungen übersehen die Demonstrant*innen jedoch jene, die legitime Kritik an der EU vorbringen und ordnen sie einfach der Seite ihrer Gegner zu", schrieb mir eine meiner Studentinnen[2], eigentlich eine EU-Aktivistin, enttäuscht. Blaue Kapuzenpullis bedruckt mit gelben Sternen. Europa-Fanclubs und Marketing-Symbole als Ersatz für EU-Politik:

---

[1] Vgl. Magali Ballatore, Thierry Blöss, *L'autre réalité du programme Erasmus*, in: Formation emploi - Revue française de sciences sociales, 103, 2008 und *Partir en Erasmus: et après ?* in: Spirale - Revue de recherche en éducation, 51, 2013.

[2] Hier sei meinen Student*innen gedankt: Was für ein Glück, solch intelligente und neugierige Menschen getroffen zu haben!

Die Entpolitisierung der europäischen Jugend wird von der EU selbst vorangetrieben. Und immer diese perverse Verdrehung der Begriffe *EU* und *Europa*. Heutzutage würde Philipp Rösler sagen: Europa ist das coolste Land der Welt.

Leider wird die deutsche Jugend nicht das Glück haben, Costa-Gavras' Film *Adults in the Room* von 2019 anschauen zu können. Er wurde in Deutschland zensiert, von keinem Filmverleih in das Programm aufgenommen und in den wenigen deutschen Rezensionen als „rückhaltlos subjektiv" bezeichnet.[3] Und dies, obwohl Costa-Gavras die Realität der Geschichte sogar geschönt hat: Christine Lagarde, heute Chefin der Europäischen Zentralbank, wird konzilianter gezeigt, als sie in Wirklichkeit ist, und Angela Merkel dämpft im Hintergrund die Aggressivität von Wolfgang Schäuble.

ILLUSION UND PROPAGANDA
Übersetzung: Solidarität und Perspektive

Ich könnte mit Hannah Arendt und Virginia Woolf weitermachen, den beiden Heldinnen meiner Jugend. Ich könnte sie aus meiner Feder ins Gespräch bringen, gerechte feministische und sogar antinationalistische Gedanken erfinden. So hätte ich es damals gemacht, als ich noch nicht in Deutschland lebte. Manchmal fühle ich mich wie Leni Riefenstahl in *Mein Afrika* oder *Die Nuba*, als sie über die Einheimischen forschte. Auch ich mag tanzende Frauen, auch ich mag *Menschen wie von einem anderen Stern*. Das war vorher, als ich mein Blut noch nicht mit den Deutschen gemischt hatte. Damals, Löcher in der Zeit.

Das war, bevor einige Begriffe durch ihre neu-artige Verwendung eine andere Bedeutung bekamen: Progressismus, Populismus, illiberale Demokratie und – Demokratie.

Ich weiß, über Demokratie zu sprechen ist vulgär. Alle kennen das Referendum von 2005, in dem die französische Bevölkerung mehrheitlich gegen die Annahme des Vertrags über eine europäische Verfassung stimmte. Alle wissen, dass das Europäische Parlament keine Macht hat, dass die Europäische Kommission die Finanz- und Haushaltsgesetze bestimmt, ohne sie vor den nationalen Parlamenten zur Debatte stellen zu müssen. Alle wissen, wie und wo man magisches Geld (dixit Emmanuel Macron) findet, um mehr Schulden zu kreie-ren. Alle wissen, dass Demokratie ein Bijou, ein Accessoire ist und dass es davon unterschied-liche Arten der Auslegung gibt. Wobei man hinzufügen muss: Die EU war von Anfang an nicht demokratisch. Und ich, seltsamerweise, verlange mit dem Altwerden mehr und mehr Demokratie von der Gesellschaft, in der ich lebe. Ich bin aber auch französisch erzogen worden.

Jeder Mensch weiß, dass die Europäische Union die Bevölkerungen verspottet. Viele wich-tige Denker*innen[4] beweisen uns seit Jahren, dass sie sich gegen die Demokratie und die sozialen Rechte stellt. Das Wort *Reform* ist ein Euphemismus für: Schluss mit dem Sozialstaat.

[3] www.german-foreign-policy.com/news/detail/8331/ (zuletzt aufgerufen am 10.7.2020).

[4] Wolfgang Streeck, François Denord, Antoine Schwartz, Andreas Wehr, Coralie Delaume, David Cayla, Frédéric Lordon, Frédéric Farah, Emmanuel Todd, les Économistes Atterrés: merci.

Heutzutage teilt man die Armut, nicht den Reichtum. Bald wird es in Frankreich wie bei den deutschen Beamt*innen sein: Streikverbot.

Menschenwürdige Renten? Da bleiben nur Sit-ins vor der Europäischen Kommission.

Wählen gehen im eigenen Land gehört zur Folklore.

Das war, bevor Alain Supiot, Rechtswissenschaftler am Collège de France, uns warnte, dass das Urteil des Karlsruher Bundesverfassungsgerichts vom 5. Mai 2020 zu Anleihekäufen der Europäische Zentral Bank ein weiterer wichtiger Schritt gewesen sei, um die absolute Hegemonie Deutschlands in der Europäischen Union zu festigen. Und als Rechtsphilosoph hat er auch immer wieder betont: Solidarität, das ist weder Versicherung noch Charity.

Das war vor der Lektüre einiger Bücher, wie *Libres d'obéir*[5] – auf deutsch: frei zu gehorchen – von Johann Chapoutot. In seinem mutigen Text zeigt er auf, wie Deutschland die Methoden des Nationalsozialismus weitergeführt und sich ein Hinterland gebaut hat (dem würden die polnischen oder ukrainischen Pflegerinnen nicht widersprechen). Das Buch handelt von Reinhard Höhn, dem ehemaligen SS-Oberführer und Gründer der Akademie für Führungskräfte der Wirtschaft in Bad Harzburg, einer symptomatischen Figur, einer himmelschreienden Allegorie für die Haltung, die Niederlage Deutschlands rächen zu wollen und zu versuchen, „sie zu sublimieren, indem man sein Land zu einem Wirtschaftsriesen macht".

Das war vor der Sondertagung des Europäischen Rats vom 21. Juli 2020, die ein weiteres Mal die neoliberalen Dogmen der EU sichtbar machte. Der Aufbauplan zur Bewältigung der von der COVID-19-Pandemie verursachten Wirtschaftskrise dient als Vorwand, um die totale Macht der Troika (Europäische Kommission, Europäische Zentralbank, IWF) zu festigen. Angela Merkel ist unsere Margaret Thatcher. Versteckt hinter den „sparsamen Vier" und ihrem vertrautesten Partner Mark Rutte hat sie ihr zweigleisiges Spiel gewonnen.[6] Die Zukunft der indirekten Entwicklungshilfe und Ausbeutungskräfte ist auf jeden Fall bis 2027 gesichert. Die anderen Länder im Osten und Süden, Frankreich inklusive, werden entmündigt, ganz im Sinne des Kabarettisten Wolfgang Neuss, der schon in den 60er Jahren formulierte: „Wir schaffen es, ohne Waffen-SS."

Auch sollten wir nicht die klaren Aussagen Manfred Webers vergessen, Fraktionschef der konservativen Mehrheitspartei EVP im EU-Parlament: Schon im Mai 2020 forderte er strenge Kontrollen mit einem direkten Durchgriffsrecht der EU auf die Daten der Empfängerländer wie Spanien oder Italien.

Struggle for life im azurblauen Himmel. *Gott mit uns*, verkleidet mit der EU-Flagge.

Wir müssen außerdem erkennen, dass die *Europafrage* ein Problem der „progressiven" Parteien wie den Grünen oder der SPD[7] ist.

5
Johann Chapoutot, *Libres d'obéir - Le management, du nazisme à aujourd'hui*, Paris: Gallimard, 2020.

6
www.bloombergquint.com/politics/merkel-says-need-to-combine-aid-with-reforms-in-signal-to-rutte (zuletzt aufgerufen am 31.8.2020).

7
Die Partei, die im Europawahlkampf 2019 mit dem Slogan „Europa ist die Antwort" antrat.

Die AfD und *le Rassemblement national* sind Symptome. Sie sind das Ergebnis von sozialdemokratischer und grüner Politik, das Ergebnis von freiwilligem Marktradikalismus, Privatisierung, Sozialabbau und der Umverteilung des Reichtums von unten nach oben.

Die EU als *supranationaler* Staatenverbund basiert auf der verpflichtenden Konkurrenz zwischen den Ländern. Sie nimmt die Gier der Investoren an und die Staatsschuld ist das Instrument der Herrschaft der Märkte. Das ist im Übrigen eine europäische Spezialität, die nicht in Japan oder in den USA existiert: Dort dürfen die Zentralbanken die Staatsschuldentitel direkt kaufen, was der Vertrag von Maastricht hier verbietet. Jean-Claude Juncker gab 2015 zu: „Es kann keine demokratische Wahl gegen die europäischen Verträge geben."[8]

Der Föderalismus der Europäischen Union führt nicht etwa zu Solidarität zwischen den Staaten, sondern ist, wie Frédéric Farah betont, ganz im Gegenteil autoritär und strafend – mit wirklichem Föderalismus hat das nichts zu tun.

Yanis Varoufakis oder Thomas Piketty sind jetzt bestimmt sehr traurig, weil sie inzwischen verstanden haben, dass Reformen innerhalb des Systems EU unmöglich sind. Die europäischen Eliten wissen das auch. Wer politisch für Demokratie und soziale Gerechtigkeit arbeiten möchte, muss die EU als ungültig deklarieren und nicht auf den Messias warten, der sowieso nie kommen wird. Er ist schon da, er heißt Martin Luther.

Das war, bevor ich einen Brief öffnete, den mir Jonas von Lenthe zu lesen gab. Darin erklärt der Jugoslawe Mirko Cvetkov seine Idee für die Europaflagge: Eine strahlende Sonnenscheibe symbolisiert unsere Zivilisation, dessen Fundament die hellenische, römische und ägyptische Kultur bildet. Mit Bitterkeit entdeckt man, in welcher geistigen Verfassung er seinen Flaggenentwurf geschickt hat. Die Zeichnung ist Ausdruck seines Wunsches nach Gleichheit, Gemeinschaftlichkeit und Frieden. Nie wieder Krieg, hieß es 1951. Wie dramatisch, wenn man die Fortsetzung der Geschichte kennt, die Jugoslawienkriege, *divide et impera*, mit Hilfe der USA, damit die jugoslawischen Teilrepubliken zur EU gehören. Die Balkanisierung Jugoslawiens wurde durch die deutsche Anerkennung Sloweniens und Kroatiens 1992 beschleunigt, gefolgt von der ersten militärischen Operation Deutschlands seit dem zweiten Weltkrieg direkt nach der Wiedervereinigung. Im Namen des Friedens entschieden Gerhard Schröder und Joschka Fischer sich 1999 im Schloss von Rambouillet für die Bombardierung:[9] *Si vis pacem, para bellum.* „Das Europa von Brüssel" war also, um Joschka Fischer von 1995 zu paraphrasieren, die Garantin des Friedens. Entsprechend liest man in offiziellen EU-Broschüren bis heute, dass Europa vor dem Krieg schützt. Zählen diese Kriege mit ihren ethnischen Säuberungen etwa nicht?

8
www.lefigaro.fr/conjoncture/2015/01/28/20002-20150128ARTFIG00441-jean-claude-juncker-pas-question-de-supprimer-la-dette-grecque.php (zuletzt aufgerufen am 31.8.20).

9
www.cairn.info/revue-etudes-germaniques-2009-2-page-471.htm# (zuletzt aufgerufen am 31.8.2020).

Wir sollten außerdem nicht vergessen, dass Europa eine Festung geworden ist, dank Angela Merkel, die die Arbeit nach der *Operation Flüchtling* im Jahr 2015 verteilt hat: die Drecksarbeit der Türkei überlassen und Hotspot-Lager für Geflüchtete auf den griechischen Inseln errichten (wodurch noch einmal die Zusammenarbeit zwischen französischen und deutschen Ingeneur*innen gefördert wird). Dann wurden auch Lager in Italien gebaut und später in Lybien. Dort werden die Geflüchteten von Frontex-Mitarbeiter*innen und den Europäischen Unterstützungsbüros für Asylfragen und anderen Subunternehmen verpflegt, Cashflow durch Sklaverei.

Die Europäische Union hat 2012 den Friedensnobelpreis bekommen. Dies ist eventuell eine Verschwörung.

Und eines Tages kam der Pastor Joachim Gauck nach Oradour-sur-Glane, dem Ort des Massakers von Oradour vom 10. Juni 1944. Und er sagte zu uns am 4. September 2013: *HEUTE IST DEUTSCHLAND EIN GUTES LAND. ES WILL EUROPA AUFBAUEN, ABER NICHT BEHERRSCHEN*

Wie kann der Politikwissenschaftler Claus Leggewie in einem Vortrag über Europas Klimapolitik behaupten, dass Ursula von der Leyen und die Europäische Kommission in ökologischen Fragen eine Vorreiterrolle übernehmen werden, wenn man die Geschichte und den Betrieb der EU – immer zum Vorteil der *Global Players* – kennt? Was tun mit diesen Widersprüchen?

Auf solche Missverständnisse trifft man auch, wenn man vergleichende Studien macht. Nehmen wir die beiden Zeitungen *Le Monde diplomatique France* und *Le Monde diplomatique Deutschland*. Serge Halimi schreibt es kristallklar in vielen seiner Editoriale: Wer Ökologie möchte, muss auf Neoliberalismus verzichten. Im März 2019 wird in *Le Monde diplomatique France* das von EU-Gegnern verfasste Dossier *Une Union à refaire*[10] veröffentlicht. Das ist in Deutschland unvorstellbar. Hier publiziert *Le Monde diplomatique* Ulrike Guérot, Macronistin und Lobbyistin der *Europäischen Republik* oder Robert Menasse, der immer wieder für weniger Hugo Boss und mehr United Colors of Benetton in der EU plädiert, anstatt die Germania Magna zu enthüllen.

Wir haben ein Problem, das seit langem keine Frage mehr ist: Über die EU sprechen heißt über Deutschland sprechen zu müssen.

Der Horizont ist nicht genug.

Der Pangermanismus hat die Farbe des Himmels und der Sterne des amerikanischen Traums, der großen Illusion.

Nicht nur der Historiker Emmanuel Todd weiß, dass die Deutschen heimlich die Amerikaner hassen. Und ich habe kein Mitleid; weder für die Patentochter von Alfred Herrhausen Carolin Emcke[11] noch für die *Le Monde*-Journalistin Sylvie Kauffmann, die beide so voller deutschem und französischem Wohlwollen sind.

---

10 www.monde-diplomatique. fr/2019/03/GUÉNOLE/59606 (zuletzt aufgerufen am 31.8.2020).

11 „Ja, aber Glück ist nicht dasselbe wie Heimat", antwortete Eva Illouz an Carolin Emcke, Carolin Emcke und Eva Illouz im Gespräch, in: 1. Spielzeitheft 2016/17, Schaubühne, Berlin.

Wir wissen, dass die deutsche Großzügigkeit nur unter Bedingungen zu haben ist.

Das wusste auch George Orwell. Es kam aber nicht bei Armin Nassehi an, als dieser 2020 ein Nachwort für Orwells erstmals auf Deutsch veröffentlichten Essay „Über Nationalismus"[12] schrieb. Viel zu dekadent, wie Europa durch die EU geworden ist, denkt Orwell, sich in seinem Grab umdrehend, das muss man erstmal erfinden! All diese Propaganda, um ein angeblich föderales Europa unter Zwang aufzubauen und mich Dinge sagen zu lassen, die ich niemals sagen wollte, hassen die Deutschen auch die Engländer? Orwell hätte niemals eine Germania Magna gewollt und er hätte für den Brexit gestimmt, im Namen der Souveränität Englands. Wie kann Armin Nassehi das Gegenteil in einem Nachwort für einen Text behaupten, den der Sozialist George Orwell 1945 geschrieben hat?

Der Skandal der EU ist die Vernichtung der Souveränität der Völker. Und sie unter dem Vorwand des Nationalismus zu zerreißen.

Dagegen verkauft uns Emmanuel Macron, *im Dienst*, in seinen Reden noch immer die französische und gleichzeitig die europäische Souveränität – scheinbar hat er vergessen, dass die Volkssouveränität nach juristischer Definition *unteilbar* ist und ebenso, dass das Selbstbestimmungsrecht der Völker zu den Grundrechten des Völkerrechts gehört.

Es ist zu spät. In Frankreich hassen alle die Polizei, in Europa hassen alle die EU und die Deutschen. Es wäre gut, wenn die Deutschen dies wüssten. Denn in Deutschland gegen den Nationalismus zu sein ist eine Verdrängung, eine Verleugnung. Die Kriegsstrategie dahinter lautet: die Souveräntitätsbestrebungen in den anderen europäischen Ländern unten halten, um den deutschen Nationalismus zu befeuern und mit diesem furchtbaren Widerspruch alle Rechtsextremen in Stellung zu bringen.

Die Bevölkerungen Italiens, Griechenlands, Spaniens und Frankreichs – das endlich akzeptieren muss, dass es zum Süden Europas gehört – wünschen sich den Ausstieg Deutschlands aus der Europäischen Union und das Ertrinken von Ursula von der Leyen.

Es ist so tragisch geworden, dass sogar Emmanuel Todd schüchtern geworden ist. Er redet jetzt nicht mehr über die Verantwortung Deutschlands innerhalb der Europäischen Union, sondern über den „Unterschied Deutschlands", obwohl wir genau wissen, dass das jüdischer Humor ist, den die Einheimischen nie verstehen werden. Lieber schauen sie die Serie *Unorthodox* auf Netflix an, um das traumatisierte Berlin als Stadt der Freiheit präsentiert zu bekommen.

Frédéric Lordon sagte, wir hätten nie eine gemeinsame Währung mit Deutschland, der verfluchten Nation, machen sollen.[13] Deutschland ist ein Monstrum, sagte Emile Durkheim 1915, ein autodestruktives Volk, das unter einer Pathologie des Idealismus leidet.

12
George Orwell, *Über Nationalismus*, mit einem Nachwort von Armin Nassehi, München: dtv, 2020.

13
Frédéric Farah, *Fake State*, Saint-Martin-de-Londres: H&O Éditions, 2020.

Vladimir Jankélévitch hat uns gelehrt, wie man Joachim Gauck zu übersetzen hat: „Die Verdrehung der Widersprüche ist seit jeher die Spezialität des deutschen Machiavellismus."[14] Nicht gegen ein Virus hätten wir einen Krieg führen sollen, wenn wir leben wollen, sondern gegen dieses Monstrum.

Der Fluch der Deutschen, das ist die Chimäre der Europäischen Union. Verflucht sind die deutschen Eliten und sie wissen ganz genau, dass Deutschsein eine griechische Tragödie ist, schlimmer vielleicht als der Niedergang des Römischen Reiches.

Die europäische Flagge ist eine Flagge für die Deutschen.

Ihre Funktion: dem Schicksal zu entkommen.

DIE FÄHIGKEIT ZUR NICHTZUGEHÖRIGKEIT

„Ich bin keine Berlinerin. Alle freien Menschen, wo immer sie leben mögen, kämpfen als Bürgerinnen und Bürger gegen diese Stadt Berlin, und deshalb bin ich als freie Frau stolz darauf, sagen zu können: Niemals werde ich eine Deutsche sein."[15]

Deutschland, Europäische Union, ich werde dein Kreuz nicht tragen und es nie mit dir teilen wollen. Zur dieser Volksgemeinschaft will ich nicht gehören, denn diese Gesellschaft hat nichts mit Europa zu tun.

Ich werde mich in Paris auf dem Cimetière du Montparnasse vor dem Grab von Émile Durkheim verbeugen und ihn trösten.

Ich werde ihm Milch und Honig bringen, bevor er sich im Grab umdreht, weil er sieht, dass die EU die neue Religion geworden ist. Die deutsche Lüge im Namen des Friedens, der Länder Europas.

Was tun? Émile Durkheim würde sagen: Waffen sammeln.

Als Frau sage ich: Liebesbriefe schreiben.

Ab jetzt werden wir nur noch Liebesbriefe schreiben.

Wir werden Liebesbriefe an Carolin Emcke schreiben.

Und eine Brücke wird immer Form annehmen über den kulturellen Gräben, welche die Bevölkerungen trennt, denn *Deutschland kann sein Schicksal, das es sich auferlegt hat, nicht erfüllen, ohne die Menschheit daran zu hindern, frei zu leben, und das Leben lässt sich nicht ewig in Ketten legen.*[16]

Marie Rotkopf, August 2020

14
Vladimir Jankélévitch, *L'imprescriptible, Dans l'honneur et la dignité*, Paris: Éditions du Seuil, 1986.

15
Frei nach der Rede von John F. Kennedy von 1963 in Berlin.

16
Émile Durkheim, *L'Allemagne au-dessus de tout*, Paris: Armand Colin, 1915.

LE SENS DU POUVOIR

> *On tourne en rond, merde, on tourne*
> *en rond, merde, on tourne...*

Francis Veber

13 colonies. 13 colonies et 13 étoiles en cercle sur un champ d'azur, le bleu du ciel du premier drapeau des États-Unis d'Amérique, un drapeau pour assembler les hommes sous un symbole, un symbole pour apprivoiser les territoires.

13 chiffre de chance. Nombre de l'accomplissement. Celui de l'indépendance, la rupture avec la vieille histoire.

Un drapeau – l'invention de la liberté. La liberté comme marque, *logos*. Un nouveau monde pour Européens rejetés, un long voyage et toujours, l'espoir. L'espoir d'un ciel bleu, de yeux de femmes.

Les plus belles inventions sont celles imaginées par les femmes, patiemment tissées, ainsi Betsy Ross, qui nous fit don d'un morceau de ses rêves en 1776, lorsqu'elle cousit le premier drapeau des USA.

12 chiffre de la mission. 12 comme les douze étoiles qui viennent couronner la tête de la Vierge Marie. 12 comme les Chrétiens. 12 comme le sang de Jésus. 12 comme la civilisation. 12 comme le commerce triangulaire. 1+2. Trinité. 12 comme les 327 réserves actuelles d'Indiens aux USA.

12 étoiles sur votre drapeau.

Heureux celui qui n'a pas de patrie; il la voit encore dans ses rêves, écrit Hannah Arendt en 1946 dans un poème presque antiromantique. Hannah

Arendt, qui n'a certainement jamais eu la nostalgie d'une *Heimat*, étrange mot inquiétant de la langue allemande, mais désirait au contraire le sentiment du sentiment, l'attachement, loin de n'importe quel territoire, car les territoires sont faits pour les enfants gâtés ou pour les Protestants perdus, voulant *l'identité* de part en part de leurs complexes d'infériorité. Les êtres libres reconnaissent la dictature des identités.

En tant que femme je n'ai pas de pays, en tant que femme je ne désire pas de pays, mon pays c'est le monde entier lui répond en écho Virginia Woolf en 1938. Elles anéantissent alors la thèse de l'appartenance, forant des trous dans le temps. Femmes sans patrie, sans pays, femmes sans identité prédéfinie, femmes universelles, genre humain sans drapeau.

1949 - 1955, Conseil de l'Europe, Strasbourg. Des hommes en quête de pardon, petits dessins, grands drapeaux couverts d'étoiles mini. La couronne de douze étoiles d'or sur fond bleu azur a été définitivement sélectionnée le 8 décembre 1955 par le Conseil de l'Europe, jour de l'Immaculée Conception, Marie, femme de pureté et d'Apocalypse.

Le drapeau est créé par le Catholique Arsène Heitz ou par le bon Juif Paul M.G. Lévy, qui avait fait vœu de se convertir au catholicisme s'il survivait à la Seconde Guerre mondiale – ce qu'il fit.

Tous ces dessins d'enfants! Regardez-les, n'hésitez pas, feuilletez le livre de l'Europe déchue. Faites-le pour vos enfants. Tous ces dessins, peints pour la bonne cause, au nom de la paix, au nom du triomphe du Bien sur le Mal, au nom de l'union des peuples.

«We need adults in the room» dit Christine Lagarde le 18 juin 2015, alors directrice du Fonds monétaire international, devant les ministres des Finances de la zone euro pendant la «crise de la dette publique grecque». Qu'est-ce que la catastrophe grecque comparée au programme Erasmus? Rien. Si Erasmus sert encore la reproduction sociale[1], la jeunesse des classes moyennes, aisées et cultivées, est toujours partie faire le tour de l'Europe, bien avant la chute du mur de Berlin.

Les slogans gaga de *Pulse of Europe* «Diffusons de l'énergie positive contre les tendances négatives!», leurs badges «Pulse together» parlent d'eux-mêmes[2]. Au lieu de réclamer de l'UE des mesures politiques concrètes, l'association allemande de Francfort *propage* les bonnes ondes de l'Union en refusant toutes critiques, et en les taxant de *populistes* ou *nationalistes*, me rapporte une de mes étudiantes[3], une activiste pro-EU un soupçon déçue. Fan club de l'Europe et sweats à capuche. Pour la jeunesse, marketing hard comme ersatz de philosophie et de politique européennes. Tout ce qui peut dépolitiser l'Union Européenne (*la politique est à la mode*) fait partie de son programme, a son département et ses conseillers, ses start-ups et Think Tanks. L'essentiel étant de détourner et fausser la terminologie et de parler d'Europe – notion géographique – alors qu'on parle

---

1

Magali Ballatore, Thierry Blöss, *L'autre réalité du programme Erasmus* in : Formation emploi - Revue française de sciences sociales, Nr.103, 2008 et *Partir en Erasmus : et après ?* in : Spirale - Revue de recherche en éducation, 2013

2

À la place, il faudrait parler de Critique de la Raison Européenne, une association de Sciences Po Paris

3

Merci à mes étudiants, quelle chance d'avoir rencontré des jeunes gens intelligents et curieux!

d'Union Européenne. Philipp Rösler, ancien Vice-chancelier, a dit un jour : l'Allemagne est le pays le plus cool du monde ! Aujourd'hui, il pourrait affirmer : l'Europe est le pays le plus cool du monde !

La jeunesse allemande n'aura pourtant pas la chance de découvrir le film *Adults in the Room* de Costa-Gavras sorti en 2019. Censuré en Allemagne, pas de salles pour sa diffusion, pas de page Wikipedia Deutsch, le film a été taxé de « subjectif sans aucune retenue » par le peu d'articles parus dans la presse allemande[4].

Or Christine Lagarde, aujourd'hui Présidente de la Banque centrale européenne, y est montrée bien conciliante et Angela Merkel, toute en retenue, semble tempérer l'agressivité de Wolfgang Schäuble. Deux femmes puissantes.

ILLUSION ET PROPAGANDE
Traduire : solidarité et perspective

Je pourrais continuer avec les deux héroïnes de ma jeunesse, Hannah Arendt et Virginia Woolf, inventer un échange féministe et même antinationaliste. C'était avant. Avant que je ne vive en Allemagne. Je me sens parfois comme Leni Riefenstahl dans *L'Afrique* ou *Les Nouba*. Comme elle je sonde les autochtones, comme elle j'aime regarder les femmes qui dansent, comme elle j'aime les hommes venant d'une autre planète. Avant que je n'aie mélangé mon sang avec les Allemands.

Des trous dans le temps. C'était avant le nouvel emploi de certains termes et par conséquent de leur signification : progressisme, populisme, démocratie illibérale – et démocratie.

Je sais, parler de démocratie est vulgaire. Tout le monde connaît le résultat du référendum de 2005 en France sur le traité de Rome II, ce *non* bafoué de la population. Tout le monde *sait* que le Parlement européen n'a en réalité point de pouvoir, que la Commission européenne décide des budgets sans rendre de comptes, sans *débat* au sein des parlements nationaux. En revanche, tout le monde *voit* où l'on peut trouver de l'argent magique, pour créer plus de dettes, ces *Schulden* – mot allemand pour dette et pour culpabilité –, et ce depuis Martin Luther comme l'a rappelé David Graeber[5]. Les dettes allemandes du XXe siècle n'ont jamais été remboursées.

Tout le monde sait donc la prétendue complexité et opacité du fonctionnement des instances de l'UE, qui ne l'est pas, complexe, puisque le système EU est conçu pour être dépendant des lois du marché. Notre démocratie est un bijou (de famille) et nous en avons plusieurs définitions, notamment aux USA.

Au commencement, l'Union européenne n'était pas démocratique. Les véritables organes dirigeants de l'Union européenne (Commission, Cour de justice, Conseil, Banque centrale) se trouvent hors de portée des voix électorales[6]. Les *pères* de l'Europe en étaient-ils conscients ?

4
www.german-foreign-policy.com/news/detail/8331/

5
David Graeber, *Dette : 5000 ans d'histoire*, Les Liens qui Libèrent, Paris, 2013

6
www.metiseurope.eu/2018/10/15/une-tribune-pour-sauver-leurope/

Étrangement en vieillissant, la démocratie est une valeur sociale qui m'est de plus en plus chère. Mais j'ai reçu une éducation française.

Tout le monde sait que l'UE raille et raye les populations. De nombreux penseurs nous prouvent depuis tant d'années[7] combien l'UE se forge contre les droits sociaux. Le mot *réforme* est devenu un euphémisme pour dire : fini l'État social. Aujourd'hui, on se partage la pauvreté, pas les richesses.

Bientôt ce sera en France comme en Allemagne ; les fonctionnaires n'auront plus le droit de grève. Des retraites décentes pour tous les travailleurs ? Sit-in devant la Commission européenne.

Voter dans son pays relève du folklore.

C'était avant qu'Alain Supiot, philosophe du droit au Collège de France, nous ait prévenu. La violence de l'arrêt du 5 mai 2020 rendu par le Tribunal constitutionnel de Karlsruhe sur la politique d'achat de dettes de la Banque centrale européenne marque une énième étape afin de maintenir l'hégémonie absolue de l'Allemagne. Cela aussi, il l'avait souligné ; la solidarité n'est ni assurance ni charité[8].

Hélas, nous savons bien au regard du XXe siècle que l'austérité tue, elle mène au fascisme, au nazisme.

C'était avant certaines lectures, et *Libres d'obéir* de Johann Chapoutot[9] m'a redonné le courage de continuer, comme les Gilets jaunes ont redonné la fierté d'être Français à Emmanuel Todd. Chapoutot montre comment l'Allemagne a perpétué les méthodes nazies du management humain après 1945 et s'est arrangée un

Hinterland, un arrière-pays – un espace annexé – à l'Est. Ce ne sont pas les aides-soignantes polonaises ou ukrainiennes qui viendraient nous contredire, ni l'anschluss de six pays des Balkans occidentaux en mai 2020, pendant la *crise de la COVID-19[10]*, alors que ni l'Allemagne ni le Nord ne venaient à l'aide de l'Italie, de l'Espagne ou de la France. Ce livre courageux est construit autour de la figure symptomatique de Reinhard Höhn, ancien SS reconverti en top ingénieur-conseil et créateur d'un célèbre institut de formation au management cultivant *les valeurs* de l'élite économique et patronale allemande. *Peut-être que nos enfants les considéreront aussi étranges et lointaines que nous apparaît désormais le jeune SS et vieux professeur de Bad Harzburg ruminant la défaite du Reich et tentant de la sublimer en faisant de son pays un géant économique.* Fin du livre.

C'était avant le 21 juillet 2020, dernier jour du Conseil européen extraordinaire, lors duquel les dirigeants de l'UE se sont mis d'accord sur un programme de relance et sur le budget 2021-2027. « Des mesures qui aideront l'UE à se reconstruire après la pandémie et soutiendront l'investissement dans les transitions écologique et numérique » selon le service communication qui a pris soin de méditer l'antinomie de l'écologique et du numérique.

7
Wolfgang Streeck, François Denord, Antoine Schwartz, Andreas Wehr, Coralie Delaume, Édouard Husson, Olivier Delorme, David Cayla, Jacques Sapir, Frédéric Lordon, Frédéric Farah, Emmanuel Todd, les Économistes Atterrés : merci.

8
www.monde-diplomatique.fr/2014/11/SUPIOT/50963

9
Johann Chapoutot, *Libres d'obéir - Le management, du nazisme à aujourd'hui*, Gallimard, Paris, 2020

10
www.consilium.europa.eu/fr/meetings/international-summit/2020/05/06/

Cet accord signe le *finishing the job* des dogmes néo-libéraux : le numérique en mode de production capitaliste ne peut nous mener sur une rive écologique. Quelle que soit la signification du virus, ce *Paket* cadeau pour la *Next Generation EU* est un prétexte honteux d'accélération de cette destruction[11]. La Troïka (Commission européenne, Banque centrale européenne, Fonds monétaire international) peut finir son travail. Angela Merkel n'est pas seulement notre Margaret Thatcher, elle est une winneuse implacable, qui sait s'entourer de ses fidèles partenaires historiques tout en jouant un double jeu, *se dissimulant derrière la France* et faisant monter au créneau le hollandais Mark Rutte[12], le frugal amant.

Les aides au développement indirectes, l'exploitation et la mise sous tutelle à l'Est et au Sud sont notre avenir jusqu'en 2027. La France sait dorénavant à qui elle doit sa *réforme* des retraites. Les gouvernements européens auront à développer leurs techniques diverses anti-soulèvements. En amont, nous avons le masque et le spectacle.

Nous garderons en mémoire le message des années soixante de Wolfgang Neuss sur la guerre économique, *Wir schaffen es, ohne Waffen-SS – nous y arriverons, sans Waffen-SS* et nous aurons à l'œil ce qui est déjà sur toutes les lèvres : l'Allemagne a son Quatrième Reich.

Struggle for life sur fond azur. *Dieu avec nous*, drapé du drapeau européen.

« L'Europe » est la solution finale des Verts et des sociaux démocrates, des partis qui n'ont de progressiste que le nom et se servant des symptômes AfD ou Rassemblement national, contre la convergence des luttes pour l'égalité. Ces mouvements politiques n'ont fait que démanteler les acquis humanistes et de justice sociale, par ailleurs très français. Le résultat de ces politiques autoritaires de soumission *volontaire* aux marchés, de privatisations, et l'idée de faire de l'UE une association supranationale basée sur l'obligation de la *concurrence* entre les États[13] permet le déchirement des populations à l'intérieur d'un pays d'abord – avec des relents fascisants utiles lors des chantages aux élections –, au sein de l'UE ensuite et enfin à l'extérieur. Chaque rivalité prend la forme du désir des investisseurs. Avec les règles d'or budgétaires d'interdiction de toutes sortes, c'est la discipline et l'expiation germanique et nordique octroyées aux populations autres. *Surveiller et punir*. Je me demande ce que Michel Foucault, adepte du sadomasochisme, aurait osé penser de l'Union européenne. Un conte cruel, comme l'écrivent Noëlle Burgi et Pierre Khalfa[14].

Jean-Claude Juncker, ancien Président de la Commission, prévenait gracieusement en 2015, « il ne peut y avoir de choix démocratique contre les traités européens ». La récente victoire d'Apple, multinationale nord-américaine à qui

11
www.lemediatv.fr/emissions/2020/crise-du-covid-19-un-pretexte-honteux-pour-continuer-lausterite-en-europe-UV9tHjg0TU-u1CprmR4nA5g

12
www.bloombergquint.com/politics/merkel-says-need-to-combine-aid-with-reforms-in-signal-to-rutte

13
Frédéric Farah, *Fake State*, Saint-Martin-de-Londres, H&O Éditions, 2020

14
L'Union européenne fait-elle le bonheur ? in : *Manuel indocile de sciences sociales*, Éditions La Découverte, Paris, 2019

l'UE avait sommé de rembourser 13 milliards d'euros d'avantages fiscaux à l'Irlande, nous éclaire en parallèle sur l'impuissance de l'association communautaire et sur sa mascarade.

Les hommes et les femmes qui travaillent pour l'UE ne construisent pas de patrie fédérale. Il n'est pas question de fédéralisme, nous rappelle Frédéric Farah, puisque le principe fédéralisme implique une vraie solidarité entre les États membres.

Pour cela, il faudrait la souveraineté populaire, qui n'est ni nationalisme ni populisme, mais la démocratie. Alors un réel *libre-échange* pourra continuer à se développer entre des pays souverains, échange qui existait avant 1993 et qui se prolongera toujours, même sans l'Union européenne[15].

Yánis Varoufákis et Thomas Piketty sont certainement bien tristes. Ils savent que les réformes sont impossibles à l'intérieur du cadre de l'UE. Les élites européennes le savent également. Qui veut travailler pour la démocratie et l'égalité sociale, donc *en prévention* de tout totalitarisme, doit déclarer l'Union européenne invalide et illégitime. Qui veut la solidarité et l'union des peuples d'Europe ne doit pas attendre le messie. Il ne viendra jamais car il est déjà là. Il s'appelle Martin Luther.

C'était avant d'ouvrir une lettre que Jonas von Lenthe a mise à ma disposition. Quelle amertume de découvrir le dessein plein d'espoir du yougoslave Mirko Cvetkov. Son projet de drapeau est un disque solaire rayonnant en honneur à notre *civilisation moderne*, dérivée de la Grèce, la Rome et l'Égypte antiques, pour lui symboles d'égalité, de collectif et de paix. *Plus jamais la guerre*, c'était en 1951. Lorsqu'on connaît la suite de l'Histoire, nous ne pouvons qu'être bouleversés par les drames qui se sont succédés, les Guerres de Yougoslavie, *divide et impera*, avec l'aide des USA, afin que les anciens pays des Balkans appartiennent à l'UE. La chute et la *balkanisation* de la Yougoslavie ont été accélérées par la reconnaissance officielle de la Slovénie et de la Croatie par les Allemands en 1992. La première opération militaire de l'Allemagne depuis la Seconde Guerre mondiale, juste après la Réunification, a lieu. Au nom de la paix, Gerhard Schröder et Joschka Fischer signent en 1999 au Château de Rambouillet le bombardement de la Serbie[16].

Si vis pacem, para bellum.

Dès lors, « l'Europe de Bruxelles », pour paraphraser Joschka Fischer en 1995, est la garante de la paix. Ces guerres comptent-elles si peu, que l'on doive lire dans les brochures officielles de l'Union européenne que « l'Europe » nous protège des guerres ?

La belle Europe de la mythologie grecque violée par Zeus. Chacun ses mythes.

Helmut Kohl a négocié un euro fort et avantageux pour son pays face à des Français naïfs, et il savait que la monnaie unique ferait de l'Allemagne une maîtresse. Le reste de l'histoire, c'est pour la presse étrangère. Il faut savoir attendre. Puis Angela Merkel, en seize ans également, a fait de l'Europe une forteresse.

15
Comme le rappelle constamment Coralie Delaume.

16
www.cairn.info/revue-etudes-germaniques-2009-2-page-471.htm

Elle est l'éthique protestante, sait diviser le travail, deale le sale boulot avec la Turquie et fait construire des camps, des hotspots sur les îles grecques. Le cynisme splendide, après son *Opération Réfugiés* de 2015, pour se dédouaner du désastre grec, croyant qu'on puisse louer en elle la fille de pasteur. Viennent d'autres camps en Italie, ils le méritent, puis l'externalisation toujours, en Libye, et la sous-traitance, pour l'agence Frontex, du cash flow pour l'esclavage.

Mais la vulgarité a une fin. Nous n'écrirons rien des programmes humanitaires et philanthropiques tel que «Compact With Africa» dont le parrain est Wolfgang Schäuble[17]. Ni sur Mayotte, la région la plus pauvre de l'UE – et de *La Grande Nation*, comme disent les Allemands en se moquant des Français, peut-être avec une pointe de jalousie, qui sait.
La paix est l'oripeau de la prochaine armée européenne – la bombe atomique allemande.
En 2012, l'Union européenne a reçu le prix Nobel de la paix. C'est éventuellement un complot.

C'était avant le Brexit.

Et un jour vint le pasteur Joachim Gauck à Oradour-sur-Glane, lieu du massacre du 10 juin 1944, et le 4 septembre 2013 il nous dit: *AUJOURD'HUI, L'ALLEMAGNE EST UN BON PAYS, ET VEUT CONSTRUIRE L'EUROPE, PAS LA DOMINER*

Comment le politologue allemand Claus Legge-wie peut-il penser que «l'Union européenne peut jouer un rôle pionnier dans la lutte contre le réchauffement climatique et l'extinction des espèces» et affirmer qu'Ursula von der Leyen prendra des décisions politiques écologiques, en connaissant l'histoire et le fonctionnement de l'UE, toujours à l'avantage des *global players*? Que faire avec ces contradictions?

D'autres *malentendus* de ce type ne manquent pas d'apparaître, il suffit de faire des études comparées: prenons *Le Monde diplomatique France* et *Le Monde diplomatique Deutschland*. Serge Halimi l'écrit clairement dans ses éditoriaux: Si l'on veut l'écologie, il faut renoncer au néolibéralisme. En mars 2019, *Le Monde diplomatique France* publie le dossier «Une Union à refaire», écrit par des opposants à l'UE. Cela est inimaginable en Allemagne, qui sait très bien ce qu'elle aurait à perdre si l'Union disparaissait. La version allemande du journal publie Ulrike Guérot, macroniste et lobbyiste de la «République européenne» et Robert Menasse, qui plaide pour toujours moins d'Hugo Boss, toujours plus de United Colors of Benetton, au lieu de dévoiler enfin la Germania Magna.

Car parler de l'Union européenne, c'est devoir ne parler que d'Allemagne.

L'horizon n'y suffit pas.

Le pangermanisme a la couleur bleue du ciel et les étoiles du rêve américain, la grande illusion.

17
www.lemonde.fr/economie/
article/2017/06/12/wolfgang-
schauble-l-afrique-doit-etre-un-
espace-de-cooperation-et-non-de-
competition_5143124_3234.html

Par-delà le marché, que les USA pilotent ou tentent de piloter l'UE est assez subsidiaire. Emmanuel Todd n'est pas le seul à savoir que les Allemands détestent secrètement les Américains. Cela ne me désole pas pour Carolin Emcke, filleule d'Alfred Herrhausen, tué vraisemblablement par la RAF, ni pour la journaliste du *Monde* Sylvie Kauffmann, toutes deux archétypes des bons sentiments français et allemand.

La générosité allemande est offerte sous conditions.

George Orwell le savait mais il n'a pas voulu le dire à Armin Nassehi, qui a écrit la postface de l'essai *Notes on Nationalism*[18] publié pour la première fois en allemand en 2020. Bien trop décadente, l'Europe sous l'UE, pense Orwell, toute cette propagande pour agencer sous la contrainte une Europe prétendument fédérale! Faire tenir à Orwell des propos qu'il n'aurait jamais dit, les Allemands haïssent-ils aussi les Anglais? Orwell n'aurait jamais acquiescé à la Germania Magna, il aurait approuvé le Brexit, au nom de la souveraineté et de l'indépendance de l'Angleterre. Comment Armin Nassehi peut-il affirmer le contraire, le croire, alors que le socialiste Orwell a écrit ce texte en 1945?

L'obscénité de l'UE réside dans l'effacement de la souveraineté des peuples. Tout en hurlant au nationalisme. Emmanuel Macron, *en service*, nous vend aujourd'hui la souveraineté française et la souveraineté européenne mais il n'est pas sans savoir qu'elle est un principe indivisible, qui plus est au nom du droit des peuples à disposer d'eux-mêmes.

Il est trop tard. En France, tout le monde déteste la police, en Europe, tout le monde déteste l'Union et les Allemands. Ce serait bien que les Allemands le sachent.

Parce qu'en Allemagne, être antinationaliste est un déni, un refoulement. De nouveau, la stratégie martiale est la suivante : étouffer les désirs de démocratie et de souveraineté des autres pays, alimenter le nationalisme allemand maquillé bleu et or et grâce à cette terrible contradiction, se servir de l'extrême droite.

Les populations d'Italie, de France – pays du Sud – de Grèce, d'Espagne… se souhaitent l'exitus de l'Allemagne et la noyade d'Ursula von der Leyen.

C'est tragique. Même Emmanuel Todd est devenu un homme timide. Il ne parle plus de la responsabilité de l'Allemagne au sein de l'UE, mais maintenant de la *différence* de l'Allemagne. Et nous savons exactement que son humour juif ne sera jamais compris par les autochtones, qui préfèrent regarder la série *Unorthodox* sur Netflix afin de voir Berlin la traumatisée se muer en ville de la Liberté.

Frédéric Lordon, à son tour un homme timide ? Ses analyses fondamentales, lorsqu'il écrit sur *cette folie*[19], que *nous n'aurions jamais dû faire monnaie commune avec l'Allemagne*, butent sur l'indicible.

L'existence de la mentalité culturelle ordolibérale, depuis Luther, intrinsèque aux Allemands. La question, ce n'est plus de savoir si l'on veut être iréniste ou non, mais de ne plus répéter les errements du passé – *Chemins qui ne mènent nulle part* – et de reconnaître enfin ces différences culturelles et anthropologiques.

[18] George Orwell, *Über Nationalismus*, postface d'Armin Nassehi, dtv, München, 2020

[19] www.monde-diplomatique.fr/2013/08/LORDON/49561

Je ne fais pas partie des irénistes, je vis en Allemagne depuis trop longtemps. Je ris lorsque Michel Serres prône la « Frallemagne », une philosophie à 50 000 Euros de l'Identity Foundation. Que ce soit avec Richard Coudenhove-Kalergi, dont on n'entend plus parler, avec des hommes bavards comme Bernard-Henri Lévy ou Daniel Cohn-Bendit, qui rêvent de faire corps avec – quoi? Le Grand Pardon? –, on s'enlise dans *la fausse conscience*, dixit Todd. C'est mal connaître les Allemands.

Quand je lis Jean-François Billeter, je philosophe sur la Suisse, son pays. Comment un homme aimant la Chine peut-il avoir l'arrogance et la bêtise de penser que nous allons fermer les yeux sur la mauvaise foi, la condescendance de l'Allemagne et que nous allons *vouloir oublier*? Comment peut-il, à son âge et en 2019, prétendre que l'on peut faire destin commun avec l'Allemagne *et* destituer le capitalisme, tout cela en citant Cicéron et tout au long d'une idéalisation à la gloire d'une Europe paternaliste[20]?

Si l'on veut sortir du capitalisme néolibéral, on doit sortir de la culture allemande.

L'Allemagne est un monstre, nous dit Émile Durkheim en 1915, un peuple autodestructeur, souffrant d'une pathologie morbide de l'idéalisme. Vladimir Jankélévitch nous avait déjà appris à décoder les mots im-mondes du président Joaquim Gauck : *le vieux machiavélisme allemand, spécialisé depuis toujours dans l'interversion des contradictoires[21]*. Ce n'est pas contre un virus que nous aurions dû faire la guerre en mars 2020, si nous voulons continuer à vivre, mais contre ce Béhémoth. La chimère de l'Union européenne est la malédiction germanique. Maudites sont les élites allemandes et elles ne le savent que trop bien : être allemand est pire qu'une tragédie grecque antique, peut-être même pire que la chute de l'Empire romain.

Le drapeau européen est pour les Allemands. Sa fonction : conjurer le sort.

LA CAPACITÉ DE NON-APPARTENANCE

« *Ich bin keine Berlinerin*. Tous les hommes libres, où qu'ils vivent, sont des citoyens qui se battent contre Berlin. Par conséquent, en tant que femme libre, je suis fière de prononcer ces mots : Ne jamais être allemande[22]. »

Allemagne, Union européenne, je ne porterai jamais ta croix et je ne la partagerai jamais avec toi. Je ne veux pas appartenir à cette communauté européenne, une société qui n'a rien à voir avec l'Europe.

J'irai au cimetière du Montparnasse à Paris et je m'inclinerai sur la tombe d'Émile Durkheim, je lui sécherai les larmes, je lui donnerai du lait et du miel avant qu'il ne se retourne, avant qu'il ne puisse voir, pourquoi l'Union européenne est la nouvelle religion, le mensonge allemand au nom de la paix, de la paix des peuples d'Europe.

20
Jean-François Billeter, *Demain l'Europe*, Éditions Allia, 2019

21
Vladimir Jankélévitch, *L'impre-scriptible, Dans l'honneur et la dignité*, Éditions du Seuil, Paris, 1986

22
D'après le discours de John F. Kennedy à Berlin en 1963

Que faire?

Émile Durkheim dirait:

Maintenant, il faut des armes.

En tant que femme je dis: Maintenant, il faut écrire des lettres d'amour.

Alors nous mettrons feu au drapeau de l'Union européenne.

Et le pont prendra toujours forme au dessus du fossé culturel qui sépare les populations, *car l'Allemagne ne peut remplir le destin qu'elle s'est assigné sans empêcher l'humanité de vivre librement, et la vie ne se laisse pas éternellement enchaîner*[23].

Marie Rotkopf, août 2020

[23]
Émile Durkheim, *L'Allemagne au-dessus de tout*, Armand Colin, Paris, 1915

Jonas von Lenthe (born 1990 in Munich) works at the intersection of publishing, curating and research. In 2018, his book *Responding to Particular Needs at a Precise Moment*, a photographic research project about the interplay of formal and informal building practices in Tirana, Albania has been published by Spector Books. He is the founder of Wirklichkeit Books, a Berlin-based publishing house focussing on works by young artists, as well as historic positions relating to poetry, play, language and art. Recent titles include a facsimile reprint of Stephanie Oursler's artist book *5 Cuts*, originally self-published in 1975 in Rome and re-edited by von Lenthe in 2021.

Marie Rotkopf (born 1975 in Paris), is an author, poet and cultural critic. She teaches the seminar *Is it possible to be against the EU?* at Leuphana University Lüneburg, and will continue as long as our democracy allows it. Her most recent books include *Fetzen. Für eine Philosophie der Entschleierung* (Scraps. Towards a Philosophy of Unveiling, with Marcus Steinweg, Matthes & Seitz, 2022), *Wie ich Rocko S. vergewaltigt habe / Comment j'ai violé Rocko S.* (How I Raped Rocko S., Ink Press, 2019) and *Antiromantisches Manifest – eine poetische Lösung* (Antiromantic Manifesto – A Poetic Solution, Edition Nautilus, 2017). She is the editor of the new edition of Émile Durkheim's last book *Deutschland über alles: Die deutsche Mentalität und der Krieg* (Germany above All: German Mentality and War), which will be published by Matthes & Seitz in 2022. Rotkopf's work is concerned with the construction and communication of power. She is interested in the rewriting of history and the poetry of the world.

REJECTED
Designs for the European Flag

EDITED BY
Jonas von Lenthe

ESSAY
Marie Rotkopf

PUBLISHED BY
Wirklichkeit Books, Berlin
info@wirklichkeitbooks.com
www.wirklichkeitbooks.com

DESIGN
We Became Aware
Valentijn Goethals & Tomas Lootens,
Louis Desmet, Lore Donckers

TRANSLATION
Nicholas Grindell (German to English,
NEW NEW ORDER)
Marie Rotkopf (German to French,
LE SENS DU POUVOIR,
AVANT-PROPOS, all letter excerpts)
Dylan Spencer-Davidson (German to English,
INTRODUCTION, all letter excerpts)

PROOFREADING
Nicholas Grindell (all English texts)
Yves-Alexandre Jaquier (all French texts)
Sophie von Lenthe (all German texts)

SOURCE OF ALL IMAGES
Council of Europe

SOURCE OF ALL LETTER EXCERPTS
Council of Europe

PRINTING
Printon AS, Tallinn

Verena Buttmann, Ulrich Genzler,
Charlotte von Lenthe, Sophie von Lenthe:
Danke für eure Unterstützung!

© 2020 Marie Rotkopf for her essay,
Wirklichkeit Books, Berlin

Third edition, 2022

First edition: 2020
Printed in the EU
ISBN 978-3-948200-03-9